The Great Garlic Book

A Guide with Recipes

Chester Aaron

Photography by
Susanne Kaspar

TEN SPEED PRESS
Berkeley, California

TEN SPEED PRESS
P.O. Box 7123
Berkeley, California 94707

Distributed in Australia by Tower Books, in Canada by Publishers
Group West, in New Zealand by Tandem Press, in South Africa by
Real Books, in Southeast Asia by Berkeley Books, and in the United
Kingdom and
Europe by Airlift Books.

Cover and interior design by Nancy Austin

Library of Congress Cataloging-in-Publication Data

Aaron, Chester.
    The great garlic book : a guide with recipes / Chester Aaron ;
photography by Susanne Kaspar.
        p. cm.
    Includes bibliographical references and index.
    ISBN 0-89815-919-9 (pbk.)
    1. Cookery (Garlic) 2. Garlic. I. Title.
TX819.G3A23   1997
641.6'526--dc21   97-19655
                                                CIP

First printing, 1997
Printed in Hong Kong

1 2 3 4 5 6 7 8 9 10 — 00 99 98 97

The Great
Garlic Book

Table of Contents

Acknowledgments

For translations from the Spanish I thank, again, Louis Segal, my (step)son, and his wife, Susan, who did yeopeople's work.

Also for translation from the Spanish, my thanks, again, to Annie Neustadter.

For translations from the Russian, my thanks to Professor Donald Fanger.

To the many chefs from Spain and Mexico and Poland and Czechoslovakia and Britain and, in the U.S., from Chicago and Marin and New Orleans and Oakland and Santa Rosa and San Francisco and Sebastopol, who responded to my requests for their favorite garlic recipes.

A special thanks to Sharon Walters and Velde Elliott at the Saint Mary's College library, in Moraga, California. Their interest and support and friendship was an ongoing joy.

A special dedication is
always in order.

This time, as in two earlier times,
the dedication is to Louis Segal,
my third arm.

A Special Acknowledgment

Here is the place and time where I offer a toast to Gilroy ranchers and to Gilroy garlic.

When I run out of my own garlics around January or February, I go to supermarkets and buy California garlic from Gilroy. I use it until my own become available in June. I do not like Gilroy's garlic as much as I like my own but hey! very few people loved my mother and father and my wife as I did.

For many years Don Christopher and all his colleagues in Gilroy continued to buck tradition, to fight floods and droughts, to experiment with soil and mulch and fertilizers, to devise new and better techniques for cultivating and harvesting, to confront bankers and critics. As young men from the prune farms and dairy ranches, Christopher and his colleagues could have continued already-proven careers, could even have gone to work in factories. They did not. They invested their labor and their love and their money in garlic, making it available to me before I began my own crusade on my own terms.

Were it not for the large growers grouping together to form the Growers Association, small growers such as myself would be ignored because there would be no ready public to appreciate our products.

A Note About the Garlics in This Book

You can, if you're lucky and self-indulgent, eat two different varieties of cultivated garlic—the hardneck and the softneck. The former, as far as I'm concerned, is much superior. However, hardnecks produce less per acre, are almost impossible to braid, demand more land and labor, and don't store as long as the softneck garlics. For all these reasons, they are not a commercially viable crop, which means that just about the only garlics you have ever found available in your supermarket are the softnecks. Still, there is a much wider, more exciting world out there for anyone willing to grow their own, as you will see in this book.

HARDNECK

Rocambole The most widely grown hardneck garlic, it is still quite difficult to grow well. The only garlic to produce a flower stalk, or scape, that forms 1 to 3 tight loops with, at the top of the scape, a sheathed cap full of tiny sterile seeds. The red-brown cloves peel more easily than do any other garlic cloves but this means a much shorter shelf life. The flavor is rich and not too hot.

ACHATAMI
Hardneck Rocambole

FLOHA
Hardneck Porcelain

Porcelain Plants can grow to 6 feet. Bulbs are clean and symmetrical with thin white wrappers. Strains vary, with 3 to 8 cloves. Skins of tall, plump cloves will vary from buff to rose to near purple. After storage, can be hotter than rocamboles.

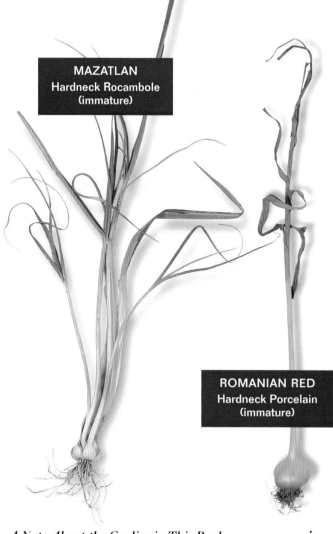

MAZATLAN
Hardneck Rocambole
(immature)

ROMANIAN RED
Hardneck Porcelain
(immature)

KITAB
Hardneck Purple Stripe
(immature)

Purple Stripe Scape can make a 270-degree curl. Wrappers of most bulbs have brighter shades of purple. Bulbs are simple to clean. The cloves, 8 to 12 to a bulb, are usually a bit smaller but peel easily. An excellent cooking garlic because it retains its taste.

PERSIAN STAR
Hardneck Purple Stripe

SOFTNECK

Artichoke Very vigorous, adaptable, and productive as well as being the easiest garlic to grow. Large bulbs have coarse thick wrappers and 12 to 20 off-white cloves. The clove skins are thick and tight, so bulbs can have a shelf life of 6 to 9 months. Appearance of the Asiatic and marbled strains, when growing, can be exotic, and their taste can be very hot.

FRENCH WHITE
Softneck Artichoke
(immature)

FRENCH WHITE
Softneck Artichoke

GUATEMALAN
Softneck Silverskin
(immature)

Silverskin Most popular of all garlics for braiding because of limber leaves, clean skin, and durability. Bulb wrappers smooth. The 12 to 40 off-white cloves are often tinged with red or pink. Clove skins are very tight, giving the garlic a shelf life of as much as a year or more. Can be very, very hot.

Creole A unique strain of the silverskin with medium to large bulbs. Beautiful scapes arch but do not circle. Cloves often colored a red so dark it's almost purple. Does well in hot, dry climates. Grown well, it can have a mild, almost sweet taste and can store longer than most hardnecks.

CREOLE
Softneck Silverskin
(immature)

CREOLE
Softneck Silverskin

PART I

Garlic Facts and Fiction

1

Six Millenniums of Alliums

800-330-5922

That's the hot line number for the Garlic Information Center.

The number was established in 1995 by a research staff at Cornell University.

Imagine: A hot line for garlic. Imagine: Garlic research at Cornell University.

There is no hot line number at Cornell or Harvard or Yale or Berkeley for onions or mint or sage or rosemary or thyme or salt or pepper.

Why?

Because everything ever said about garlic is true. Even the lies.

Garlic has been loved and occasionally (but rarely) scorned for more than 6,000 years.

No other herb (some call it a vegetable) has served as many roles in the culinary and medical and folkloric histories of so many cultures.

Fresh cloves, garlic teas, syrups, tinctures, powders, tablets, pills have been used as: an aphrodisiac; a treatment for colds, flu symptoms, coughs, earache, fever, bronchitis, shortness of breath, sinus congestion, headache, stomachache, high blood pressure, atherosclerosis, hypertension, diarrhea, dysentery, gout, rheumatism, whooping cough, pinworms, ulcers, and snakebites; as food; as protection against every possible evil, real or imagined.

Identified in garlic and its oils are thirty-three sulfur compounds, seventeen amino acids, plus germanium, selenium, and a variety of other minerals, as well as vitamins A, B_1, and C.

History, historians tell us, is based on facts. History, cynics tell us, is written by the winners.

Fact The tomb at El Mahasna, in Egypt, preceding the reign of the first Pharaohs, was constructed in 3750 B.C.

OK, so that's 5,747 years ago, not quite 6,000.

When archaeologists discovered the tomb in 1911, they found inside detailed models of garlic bulbs. The bulbs consisted of long coils of unbaked but whitewashed clay wrapped around a clay core. There was no possibility of doubt. They were catalogued as garlic bulbs.

The still-prevailing theory: The garlic models had been placed near the sarcophagus to ward off evil, to guarantee the soul of the saint or hero interred there a safe journey through eternity.

Fact The Pharaoh Tutankhamen reigned about 2,000 years after the tomb at El Mahasna was constructed. That was 4,000 years ago, give or take a century or two. When, fifty years ago, archeologists opened Tutankhamen's tomb, they discovered, almost lost among the precious gems, the statuary, and the silver and gold, six dried but perfectly preserved heads of garlic. Not models of garlic, but garlic. The real thing.

Fact Around 1500 B.C. the architect Kha, a near contemporary of Tutankhamen, began his casual drift into eternity. He could not have known then (or did he?) that

some 3,000 years later his tomb would be precisely re-assembled at the Egyptological Museum in Turin, Italy.

Being an architect instead of a Pharaoh, Kha possessed no coffers of gold and silver, no carved sarcophagus inlaid with precious gems. Accompanying him into the afterlife: pieces of furniture; a variety of kitchen utensils; an intricately woven basket filled with a small collection of foodstuffs that included...you guessed it...garlic.

Fact Midway through the fifth century B.C., the famed historian, Herodotus, visited the Great Pyramid of Cheops at Giza. Being an historian, he noted his discoveries in his journals.

> There is an inscription in Egyptian characters on the pyramid which records the quantity of radishes, onions and garlic consumed by the laborers who constructed it; and I perfectly well remember that the interpreter who read the writing to me said that the money expended in this way was sixteen thousand talents of silver...

Fact Herodotus was not available to record the trials and tribulations of the Israelites when they labored for the Pharaohs of the New Kingdom and, later, wandered for forty years through the desert.

These wandering tribes, it is written, longed for manna.

Wrong. The wandering tribes longed for garlic.

> The rabble who had joined the people were overcome by greed, and the sons of Israel themselves began to wail again, "Who will give us meat to eat?" they said. "Think of the fish we used to eat free in Egypt, the cucumbers, melons, leeks, onions and garlic! Here we are wasting away, stripped of everything; there is nothing but manna for us to look at!"

NUMBERS: 11: 4-6

Fact As today, garlic in ancient (and not-so-ancient) times, has had its detractors.

Perhaps the greatest poet of them all, ode man Horace, complained about the smell of garlic. He insisted that the herb was more poisonous than hemlock. Only vulgar lowlifes, he said, would consume garlic.

Leaping ahead here momentarily, to a **Fact** four (three?) thousand years after the death of Horace. In 1938, a committee from the United States Department of Agriculture, was evaluating the benefits of establishing a garlic trade. The consumption of garlic, the committee reported, was restricted...

> ... to the needs of the Mediterranean races,
> the main markets being New York, Chicago and
> St. Louis.

Mediterranean races: the then-current vulgar lowlives.

Garlic, the committee concluded, could never be an important commercial item in the United States of America because the Mediterranean races would never be important in the United States.

Fact A Mohammedan legend has it that when Satan departed the Garden of Eden after the fall of Man (and Woman), garlic sprang up from the spot where he placed his left foot. In the spot where he placed his right foot: onions.

Fact Before Mohammed, before the Old Testament, before Horace, the poet Homer was regaling his audience with lyrics about how Ulysses, thanks to his "Yellow Garlick," outwitted the evil Circe, thus avoiding the fate of his unfortunate comrades who, not possessing "the Yellow Garlick," had been turned into swine.

Fact The Romans, like the Greeks, honored garlic, devoutly certain that the aromatic herb gave their soldiers strength and courage. Along with the violets and roses the Roman legions planted around the walls of their fortresses and villas (on the European mainland and in Celtic Britain), they planted garlic.

Ever since, perhaps in protest, perhaps in defiance of foreign invaders, British fashion as well as British cuisine has been in rebellion. The word for *bland* in both English and Latin is *bland*.

> What do you think? Young women of rank eat—
> you will never guess what—garlick!
>
> THE POET PERCY B. SHELLEY,
> AFTER A VISIT TO FRANCE.

Unless very sparingly used, the flavor of garlic is disagreeable to the English palate.

A WARNING IN MRS. BEETON'S COOKBOOK, **THE VICTORIANS' KITCHEN BIBLE.**

Fulder and Blackwood, in *Garlic—Nature's Original Remedy* (Healing Arts Press, 1991) write that

> ...the Buddah's most senior disciple, Sariputra, cured himself of an upset stomach by eating garlic; thus Buddhist monks are allowed it as a medicine. However they are not officially allowed it as a food for fear of upsetting the other monks.

Louis Van Deven, in his *Onions and Garlic Forever* (Louis Van Deven, 1992) citing *The People's Chronology*, states that

> ...in 1274 Marco Polo visited the Chinese city of Yunnan and saw the 'Tartars' eating raw beef, mutton, buffalo, poultry and other flesh, chopped and seasoned with garlic.

The facts go on and on: the early Sumerian diet included garlic; the *Shih Ching* (the Book of Songs), a collection of traditional ballads said to have been written by Confucius, lauds garlic; in the eighth century B.C., garlic was found growing in the gardens of the King of Babylon; the Phoenicians and the Vikings packed garlic into their sea chests to sustain them over long voyages. Etc., etc., etc.

Fact finale: Albert Schweitzer is reported to have used garlic in Africa to combat cholera, typhus, and amoebic dysentery.

2

A Consideration of Taste

Dominic's parents arrived in America, from Italy, two years before the twentieth century began. Ten years later, on their sheep ranch in Bodega, in Northern California, in the southwest corner of the field behind their newly built American house, Dominic's parents planted thirty garlic cloves they'd bought from a relative who'd been in America just long enough to acquire the necessities for immigrant survival.

Every year since then, in the second week of every October, not thirty but 100 cloves of garlic have gone into the same garden in the same field behind the same old house.

Last year, Dominic, now over seventy years old, planted not the now-traditional 100 cloves, but 200. Half of that number were descendants from Dominic's father's first planting, a variety common to California; common, in fact, to the entire United States. It is called *California garlic*, or *California Early*, or *California Late*.

The extra 100 cloves Dominic planted for the first time last October are descendants from eight varieties of garlic selected from the fifty-five varieties of garlic I grow on my small farm in Occidental, about ten miles from Dominic's sheep ranch.

CALIFORNIA EARLY
Softneck Artichoke

Originated in California, where it is grown commercially. Very vigorous and productive. Large bulbs averaging 10 cloves. Generally mild but can be hot after long storage.

I had wrapped two heads of each of those eight garlics in special paper and presented them to Dominic just after Christmas dinner.

Dominic opened one of the packages, lifted one of the heads, peeled away the outer layers of white skin, and threw back his head, as if a fist had sprung out of the wrappings. "Hey," he said, "this garlic is red."

He held up the now-naked head, disclosing to his wife and children and grandchildren a collection of cloves dressed not in white skin but red. Dark red. Dark blood-red.

With grave suspicion, Dominic glanced from the red clove to me, as if I were trying to trick him. "Did you spray paint these cloves?"

"Pull one loose," I said. "Taste it."

He pried a single clove from the head and when he picked up a knife to pry the skin loose, I said, "No, no. Just squeeze the clove."

When he squeezed with thumb and forefinger the skin broke free.

"That," I said, "is why chefs like to use this garlic. It's called Spanish Roja. It's easy to peel and saves time and money. Taste it, Dominic."

He grabbed the naked white clove between his teeth, bit off half of it, and chewed. He shook his head, as if it were suddenly filled with fog or spider webs.

"This ain't garlic," he said. "This is cake."

After tasting Spanish Roja, Dominic opened the remaining packages, to taste, in order, Creole

SPANISH ROJA
Hardneck Rocambole

Seed stock from Filaree Farm. A Northwest heirloom brought to Portland area before 1900. Performs poorly in mild winter climates. Best selling ophio (hardneck) garlic. Described as "the most piquant garlic in the world" and "when well grown its flavor describes true garlic." In taste tests Spanish Roja is often in the top two with Creole Red. Very easy to peel.

THE GREAT GARLIC BOOK

Red, Polish Carpathian Red, Russian Red Toch (from the Republic of Georgia), Persian Star (from Samarkand, Uzbekistan), Inchelium Red (from the state of Washington), Chesnok Red (from Shvelisi, Republic of Georgia), and Armenian (from the village of Hadrut Karabagh).

Dominic, following consumption of the eighth garlic, poured us both a glass of his homemade red wine and made me an offer I couldn't resist.

He intended to plant these garlics, but if, after next summer's harvest, I were to give him samples of eight more garlics, so he could plant them the following October, I could, every spring and fall, share with him and his family the wild mushrooms that grow in glorious abundance in his fields, under the oak and fir trees. Garlic and mushrooms. The only combination that might be superior would be garlic and more garlic.

Now, as to taste. Taste is as personal as your name. Or mine. Taste, like names, varies. As an example, I selected one garlic, Spanish Roja. The *probable* origin of the variety of garlic called Spanish Roja is, obviously, Spain. (Note that I stress *probable* .)

Ron Engeland, at Filaree Farm in Okanogan, Washington, tells us that when well-grown, the flavor of Spanish Roja describes true garlic. I agree with Engeland on most things but especially on this.

For me...remember, I say, *for me*...Spanish Roja has a moderately strong bite; meaning it is moderately hot on the tongue. But the heat fades fast, leaving the earthy garlic's distinct taste (not the heat but the taste) to settle at the back of the throat.

You or your mate, or your guests, might have a response different from mine.

In garlic taste-tests across the country Spanish Roja has traded first and second place with Creole Red.

The skin on the cloves of Creole Red can be even darker than the skin on the cloves of the Spanish Roja, a red occasionally so dark it is almost purple, vying in beauty with the red on Burgundy or Xian garlics.

For me, Creole Red has an earthy taste that is almost sweet.

CREOLE RED
Softneck Silverskin

Seed stock from Filaree Farm. Medium-sized heads with two or three layers of striking, solid purple cloves. May turn lighter pink in northern climates. Flavor is mild, sweet. In taste tests, trades first or second position with Spanish Roja.

Have you ever witnessed a wine tasting, where so-called experts sit and debate the qualities of the various offerings and then try to agree on the factors that make one wine superior to all others?

Have you heard *aficionados* compare cigars?

Prepare to defend yourself against assault if you ever attend a festival in the Republic of Georgia and witness three families comparing the taste and virtue of their individual garlics, inherited within the clans through a span of fifteen or twenty generations. Don't, if you value your life, take sides.

The eleven garlics mentioned so far—Armenian, Burgundy, California White, Chesnok Red, Creole Red, Inchelium Red, Persian Star, Polish Carpathian Red, Russian Red Toch, Spanish Roja, Xian—are as different from each other as Fume Blancs are different from Pinot Noirs, or Merlots from Zinfandels. The various garlics differ as do the grapes mixed and matched to produce the many different wines.

Think: why would the wine of a certain year be more highly prized than the same wine of an earlier (or later) year? Why (and how?) are French wines compared to California wines? California to New York? U.S. to Australian?

At dozens of garlic taste tests that I have conducted, chefs, food lovers, and food writers have always expressed surprise at the display of the various garlics I spread across the table. As sophisticated, as cosmopolitan, as learned as they were, they had been unaware that there was any garlic but that white turban-shaped collection of cloves available in the bins of every supermarket in the country.

"Come on, all garlic tastes the same."

Do the nay-sayers, the cynics, the doubting Thomases and Thomasinas, have this attitude toward the hundreds of potential combinations of grapes that shape one or another of the hundreds of wines available all over the world?

"Not!" my students would say, with a sneer of superiority.

Once the suspicious participants enter into the garlic tastings, comparing one variety to another, to a second and a third and a fourth, they usually beg for two or three of their favorite varieties to take home. Price is no deterrent.

Selecting *the best* is never a practice in unanimity or even democracy. No matter how cynical or skeptical the guests at the various taste tests, the great majority have always, without fail, conceded, at the end of the event, that, yes, there is a wide

BURGUNDY
Softneck Silverskin (Creole Group)

Seed from Filaree Farm. Creole Group includes Ajo Rojo and Creole Red. Source uncertain, possibly France and/or Germany. Bulbs moderate to large size, with 8 to 12 cloves covered with very striking burgundy skins. Biting heat that fades slowly.

span of taste in the four or ten or twenty garlics just offered. And there is always, eventually, a concession that the standard, traditional, omnipresent supermarket garlic is not in the same league with these fancy garlics, these special garlics, these *new* garlics.

Last year, at an agriculture conference at Big Sur, California, I met a representative from one of the huge, extremely successful commercial garlic ranches in Gilroy. "Look," she said, "let's understand something before we make our presentations. I'm familiar with your garlics. You're familiar with mine. I know that if there are ten garlics presented for tasting, and nine are yours and the tenth is our California Late or California Early, your nine garlics will come in first through ninth. Our California Early or California Late will come in tenth."

I demurred, saying well, it might not be tenth.

She did not know that she could very well have been describing a 1993 taste test conducted at Oliveto Restaurant in Oakland, where I'd presented not ten but twelve of my garlics to a gathering of fifty prominent people involved in one way or another with food, certainly with the use of garlic. The thirteenth garlic, as a base, was the familiar California Late. Four of my twelve were softnecks, eight were hardnecks. Rated number one: Spanish Roja. Rated number two: Creole Red. Number three: Russian Red Toch. The California Late was indeed ranked thirteenth.

It's important, regarding the concept of taste, to consider events subsequent to that 1993 taste test.

The garlics that were ranked high at that taste test did not achieve the same rank at a follow-up taste test two years later at the same restaurant. Nor were the rankings of 1993 and 1995 at those taste tests similar to the rankings at a taste test at the Culinary Institute in

RUSSIAN RED TOCH
Softneck Artichoke

Seed from Filaree Farm. Originally from the village of Tochliavri in Republic of Georgia. Very large rose-tinged bulbs. Cloves are streaked medium to light with red and pink. Raw taste described as perfect garlic flavor.

ROMANIAN RED
Hardneck Porcelain

Seed from Filaree Farm.
Came to British Columbia from
Romania. Bulbs moderately
large, with 4 to 5 cloves
streaked and lined on buff
brown background. Hot and
pungent flavor with healthy,
long-lasting bite. Very long
storage.

Saint Helena in 1996, even though, again, the same garlics were presented.

Taste varies.

But so do garlics.

So do most crops, most foods.

Each of us has a body chemistry, and hence a taste response, as varied and unique as our fingerprints. That is why taste varies from individual to individual. That is why I describe taste, in garlics, with reluctance, always with caveats. I always add *for me*. I love the Fameuse apple, while most people find it beautiful, but not sweet enough. I like a fine merlot; many winers and diners grimace when offered a merlot. "Might as well drink grape juice."

For those of you who smoke cigars, compare a Royal Jamaica to a Hoyo de Monterey. Next compare a Hoyo de Monterey from any *finca* in Venezuela to a Hoyo de Monterey from Cuba. Now compare a 1997 Hoyo from Cuba to a (should you be so fortunate to have one) pre-Revolutionary Hoyo from Cuba and you will groan. With resentment.

The knowledgeable Cuban would sniff at the green cigars Americans love; he/she takes a *maduro* so dark it's black, oozing nicotinic oils. Delicious! I'll trade all my Transylvanian garlics for one pre-Revolutionary Hoyo de Monterey.

Taste is in the eye of the beholden.

Were my Romanian Red garlics, for example, served to two people for tasting, even if half of the same single clove were given to each of the two, there could be two reactions, two different descriptions. One person might say the Romanian Red is hot, the other might say it is, well, not very mild; one might say it has

CHET'S ITALIAN RED
Softneck Artichoke

Seed from Horace Shaw via Filaree Farm. From abandoned garden site in Tonasket, Washington. Very large bulky bulbs with 10 to 20 cloves in 4-clove layers. A good raw garlic for people who want solid but restrained, even mild, garlic flavor. Tends to be hot where winters are cold and long.

a slight odor, the other might say it is extremely pungent; one might say the bite, or heat, is brief and then fades, the other might say the bite is long-lasting and burns the tongue and palate like a Jalapeño pepper.

Because taste, when responding to garlic, is related to heat, let's talk briefly about heat.

Compared to other herbs, garlic's taste is distinct because it is often affected by a "reflex taste," meaning a reaction to heat, a remnant of the original impact, a faint reminder of the first meeting of garlic and lips, of garlic and tongue, of garlic and palate, of garlic and throat.

Some garlics, like peppers, are definitely hotter than others. But, as with peppers, the heat varies not so much in degree as in quality. One garlic's heat will explode in your mouth and linger (Metechi or Romanian Red); another's heat will build slowly, explode, then dissipate (Zemo, from the Republic of Georgia, or Russian Red Streak); the garlic called Floha (from Germany), will be fiery; another garlic will (usually but not always) be so mild as to be almost sweet (Inchelium Red, from Washington, or Chet's Italian Red, also from Washington, or Guatemalan Ikeda, from the province of Huehuetenango.)

All of this said, I now have to inform you that other...other and uncontrollable...factors complicate even further the process called *taste*. For example, an Arkansas Black apple grown in my soil and in my weather conditions will not taste the same as an Arkansas Black grown on the same tree last year. It will not taste the same as an Arkansas Black grown where, in contrast to the mild winter temperatures at my farm, there are each winter, fifty or sixty days of freezing temperatures.

What, for example, was the composition of the soil in which the specific garlic was grown? The weather? Were the summers mild or hot? Were the winters moderate or extremely cold? Was the garlic under stress when growing, meaning long periods of drought and/or heat and/or long periods of rain? Was the garlic harvested at its peak or had it remained in the soil too long? Did it lie in the sun for days after harvest or was it removed, immediately after it left the ground, to the shade? Once harvested, how was the garlic stored? In cool temperatures? Did it hang, or "cure," for a week, a month, two months? Were the stalks cut before curing? After? How long had the garlic lain in the market bin before purchase and how long, after being brought into the kitchen, had it rested on the kitchen shelf in an open container above the stove to dehydrate?

One or a combination of this multiplicity of factors can affect the taste of the garlic clove.

Example: A Siberian garlic grown in California might (almost certainly will) taste different from the Siberian garlic grown in its native Siberia; my Siberian will probably taste different from the Siberian grown by Ron Englund at Filaree Farm, 900 miles to the north, in the state of Washington. It could even taste different from the Siberian garlic I grew last year or will grow next year.

INCHELIUM RED
Softneck Artichoke

Seed from both Filaree Farm and David Cavagnaro at Seed Savers Exchange. From Colville Indian Reservation in state of Washington. Considered by some to be the oldest garlic in North America. In 1990 at a taste test at Rodale Gardens, was rated top softneck. Denser and heavier than most garlics. Not easily peeled. Mild but lingering flavor; can sharpen with storage.

A suggestion, should you be moved to use or plant your own garlic (as I will soon be advising you to do): Test the varieties of garlic in the local farmer's markets where garlic is available each season, select those varieties that pass your own taste tests, keep some cloves to eat, keep others (the largest, fattest, healthiest) to plant.

If, like most Americans, you cannot, will not, eat garlic raw, try it roasted. But be prepared: when boiled or roasted, almost all garlics lose their bite, their taste becomes quite nutty and the qualities that distinguish the taste of one garlic from another are diminished or even neutralized. The tastes do vary but over a narrower span than when they are used raw or sautéed or fried.

Try the garlics on vegetables, on meat, on pasta, on seafood, on toast, in stews, in soups, in salads. A garlic that does not please you when used on vegetables might raise you to ecstasy when used in a soup. A garlic that sets your teeth on edge when raw might be velvety smooth on the tongue when incorporated into salads or sauces, or on bruschetta.

Back to taste.

The following can help . . . only *help* . . . simplify the problems when you see, taste, plant the various garlics.

Is the garlic that you liked a hardneck or a softneck? Ask your seller. Demand an answer.

If it's a hardneck, is it a variety called Rocambole?

SIBERIAN
Hardneck Purple Stripe

Seed from Filaree Farm. Large bulbs with beautiful blue to purple-veined skin covering 5 to 7 fat, dark brown cloves. Secured originally by fishermen trading green leafy vegetables with peasants. Strong flavor, quite hot.

THE GREAT GARLIC BOOK

Porcelain? Purple Stripe? A sub-variety of Purple Stripe called Marbled? If it's a softneck is it a Silverskin? Is it an Artichoke garlic?

Wait a minute. A garlic is not an artichoke.

Patience. Stay with me now, more details will arrive later.

The hardneck garlic (*Allium ophioscorodon*), the closest descendant of wild garlic, produces a flower stalk (called a *scape*) and is likely to produce a smaller bulb (compared to a softneck) underground, should that stalk, or scape, not be cut when it appears. Below ground, a single circle of cloves forms around this hardneck's central stalk. The stalk will often curl, and then curl again, as it grows above ground. A cluster of small garlic cloves (bulbils) will develop inside the sheath at the top of the scape.

Botanists and plant pathologists suspect that softneck garlic (*Allium sativum*) probably evolved from hardneck garlics and, in that evolution, have partially lost the ability to send up a flower stalk, though they can bolt when stressed. Though softneck garlics are usually easier to grow, and are, in fact, the most widely grown garlics in the world, they sometimes lack the near-wild flavor of the hardnecks, verging often on being very hot or very mild. Compare, for example, the taste of the domestic mushrooms available in your supermarket to the taste of a wild *Boletus edulis* or chanterelle or morel.

Each of the different hardneck varieties (Purple Striped, Porcelain, and Rocambole in the hardnecks; Artichoke and Silverskin in the softnecks) has a unique character. Though form and shape of stalks and leaves, size and appearance of bulbs, size and shape and number and color of cloves are repeated in successive generations, there will be occasional mutants. The unique qualities of each variety are reproducible, though each variety is likely to best follow its genetic map, performing to its ultimate and distinct authority, in certain soils and certain climates.

The softnecks have more appeal to both the kitchen cook and the professional chef because (in ideal conditions) they store better and longer, often for ten or twelve months. Most of the fifty-five hardnecks I grow begin to show deterioration four to six months after harvest, having reached (in my estimation) the peaks of their varied tastes in their second or third month. From there, even though it's all downhill, they still, in my mind, are superior to their cousins in the bins of your local supermarket.

ARMENIAN
Hardneck Rocambole

Seed from Silva Baghdassarian, in the Armenian village of Hadrut Karabagh. One of the largest bulbed and most intense garlics in my collection. Bulbs firm and white with rose to purple stripes. Extremely tough and durable leaves and stalks. Strong, earthy flavor. Ideal for roasting. One of my favorites.

My own taste tests have convinced me that of the fifty-five different garlics I grow, there are four that continue to be exceptional, with another four or five closing in. Those four: Armenian, Russian Red Toch, Xian, with Spanish Roja trading positions with Creole Red. See if you can decide which is a hardneck, which a softneck.

Many other growers believe that certain strains of the softneck garlics, when well grown, are the equal of Rocamboles in flavor. My response? Their taste is in their cloves.

All of the foregoing advice regarding taste is judiciously composed of broad generalities. You might find an occasional strain superior to others, a strain I or others consider only fair. Stay with your choice because, if you grow a few, each new harvest will offer you unpredictable and therefore exciting nuances not necessarily available the previous season or the next.

After this introduction to garlic taste...and this is important...I now suggest that your choice of the garlics you bring into your kitchen ought not be made on the basis of taste alone. Equally important is your lifestyle.

XIAN
Hardneck Purple Stripe

Seed from Filaree Farm and an unknown lady in San Francisco's Chinatown. A very rare garlic from northeastern China. Tall, thick stalks and wide, heavy leaves. Very large bulb with thumb-sized cloves covered with purple-red, almost black skin. Taste is not too hot but very rich. One of my favorite garlics.

How do you prepare your foods? What kinds of food? How do you store your garlic? Given your space, your free time, your kitchen habits, your culinary needs, one or another garlic might be more...not necessarily desirable...but fitting. You might find that though you prefer the taste of a California Late your family might think it too hot, so you compromise and try to locate (to eat or to plant, or both) an Inchelium Red from Washington or a Guatemalan or a garlic called Chet's Italian Red.

Should you grow your own garlic, the adaptability of the many different garlic varieties to your soil, your weather, your available time, becomes as important as taste or shelf life. You cannot predict the result; you can only, each season, compare.

Remember above all that garlic is a food.

Eat it.

It is almost totally free of calories (about two per clove) and totally free of fat and very low in sodium.

Eat it. Love it. The odds are very high that garlic will...well, almost always...love you in return.

Can you say that about thyme? About sage? About arugula? About your child?

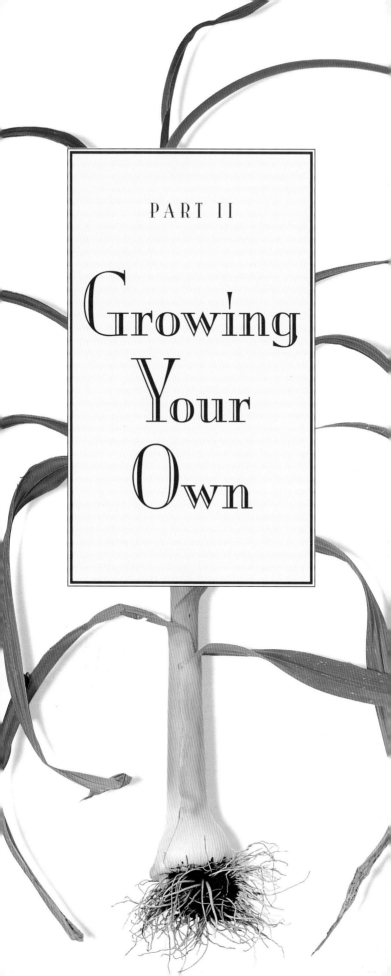

PART II

Growing Your Own

3
Growing Garlic on Your Own

Let's start with the assumption that you love or will love garlic.

Let's start with another assumption: you live in a third-floor apartment in the center of the city. Your apartment has a small deck that receives sun seven or eight hours a day, on those days when the sun shines.

Why, you've often wondered, or are about to wonder, why don't I grow my own garlic?

Your options for growing garlic are much more limited than your options for eating garlic. But be patient. All problems have solutions, sometimes more than one.

On the deck of your apartment you should be able to grow as much or more garlic than you can eat in a year.

When you inherit that chunk of money from your long forgotten aunt/uncle you will give up your apartment and purchase a two-story house in exurbia, beyond suburbia. The large yard behind that house receives seven or eight hours of sun a day, on those days when the sun shines.

But for now you have this third-story apartment and its miniature deck to contend with.

Well, we take pleasure where it finds us.

It is late summer. Running about through the city you happen onto a farmer's market where a vendor offers four crates on a counter, each crate filled with what the vendor says are different *kinds* of garlic. Meaning, you will discover, if you haven't already, different varieties.

None of the four varieties available in those crates is at all like the garlic you have used all your life, that your mother, father, sister, brother, have used all their lives. The heads (or *bulbs*) of three of the garlics appear to be much larger than the heads of garlic available in your supermarket. One is smaller. Two of the four are rounder, one is flatter than your familiar garlic. One is so oddly shaped as to be neither round nor flat.

One of the heads is wrapped in red skin, one in crisp brown, two in skins that disclose distinct purple stripes. The oddly shaped bulb, the one in the brown skin, is twice the size of your fist. Cloves cling to the outer walls like determined but somewhat malformed stowaways.

Hand-printed signs on each of the four crates inform you that two of the garlics are from Russia, one is from France, one is from Spain. The vendor, a kind, well-meaning person, can give you no more specific information. He is telling you what he was told when, last year, at one or two or three farmer's markets in other cities, he purchased the previous generation of these garlics.

"They're different." That's the extent of his pitch.

Neither you nor he realize that the country's name is not the name of the variety but merely the country in which that specific garlic was found. It might or might not be native to that country.

Well, you are a card-carrying member of your generation. You are interested in different things. In new things. New cars, new computers, new clothes. New recipes.

You have been receiving a variety of magazines, several devoted to food. For months you've been reading about these fancy garlics, these *exotic garlics*, these *new garlics*.

Here they are in these crates, in this market, in your neighborhood.

Neither you nor the vendor knows that these garlics did not just fall off the turnip truck. They have been available, to monarch and peasant, to soldier and slave, for thousands of years—6,000 at least. Remember?

Prudent, but courageous, as well as optimistic, and also curious, you select two heads of garlic from each of the four crates and solicit advice from the vendor regarding taste. And tips, should you eventually be so moved, for growing the garlic. An unlikely eventuality, given your circumstances. The only things you've ever grown is inches. And pounds. Also your thumb is black, from the tip of the nail to the first knuckle.

Over the next few days you prepare a variety of dishes for yourself and your friends, using one and then another of the garlics. You discover that not only do none of these garlics taste like the supermarket garlic

Kitab (immature)

Kingdom	Plant
Division	Anthophyta
Class	Monocotyledones
Superorder	Liliiflorae
Order	Asparagales
Family	Alliaceae
Genus	*Allium*
Species	*sativum*
Subspecies	*ophioscorodon,* *sativum*

Hardneck varieties (*ophioscorodon*):
> Purple Striped
> Porcelain
> Rocambole

Softneck varieties (*sativum*):
> Artichoke
> Silverskin

you've been using all your life, but no matter the order in which you test them, not one of the four tastes like the other three.

There are also physical variations among the four varieties: one has eight fair-size long, narrow cloves, tucked around an inner core of several tiny cloves; another has only four cloves, total, but each of those four is very large and very fat; the cloves of the third are loose, separate, almost free-standing; the cloves of the fourth tightly hug the body of the head, curving up and around like the leaves of an artichoke. Artichoke? Artichoke. Remember?

You are Columbus, bound for the New World; you are an astronaut, departing your missile to walk in space and explore the surface of the moon. The difference: This trip doesn't cost the taxpayer a penny. It's free. Well, relatively free.

Following the advice of the vendor and then of a reliable aide at your nursery...yes, you now decide to try, no matter the size of your apartment and your deck, you intend to grow your own garlic...you've eaten the small and medium cloves from each of the four varieties and you've saved the biggest, fattest cloves for planting. You'd remembered to follow advice to store them in individual paper bags, each bag marked with the name of its enclosed variety.

"You'll need planters," your nursery aide reminds you. "How many cloves did you save?"

"Four cloves from each head. A total of sixteen."

The gardener has on hand the September '96 issue of *Sunset* magazine, which contains an article that not only praises these new, non-traditional garlics but, on the last page, offers simple directions about how they should be planted and nursed on their way to harvest.

"You'll need four planters. One for each variety. Four cloves to each planter. Here are four plastic tags. Label them, identifying each variety. Stick the tags in the soil so you'll be sure which planter has which garlic."

Three of the four planters you've bought at the nursery are twenty-four inches tall and twenty-four inches square. One, a circular ceramic pot, is twenty inches in diameter.

Because you don't want the planters to crash through your deck onto the neighbor sitting in his/her chair on the deck below, you place your planters at various strategic locations to catch the maximum amount of sunlight but not stress the underlying girders. You don't have homeowner's insurance, nor does the owner of the apartment house.

When, you ask, do you plant?

The time-to-plant depends on the state or country in which you live. If your winter is sure to bring freezing temperatures, you'll be planting three to four weeks before the first predicted frost, so the roots have time to establish themselves. In areas of mild winters, you'll be planting anytime between mid-October and late November.

Your deck is not a 30,000-acre ranch in Gilroy, California, so you won't have to buy a tractor. You would be wise to buy a set of gardening tools, those oversized forks and spoons. You'll be using your fingers a lot, so if you are the dainty type, you might need gloves.

Don't concern yourself too much about soil for so small an enterprise. For these planter boxes you'll buy about 200 pounds of what the genius at your nursery calls "good soil." You, or someone else, will have to haul four heavy bags on the elevator to the third floor.

The aide at the nursery: "Oh, along with the soil, you'll need...let's see, for sixteen cloves...you'll need a half pound of bone meal. Sorry, it only comes in one-pound bags. Save a half pound for next year."

After you fill your planters with soil you follow the advice in that September '96 issue of *Sunset* magazine, soaking the soil well without flooding it.

Using whatever tool you have available (as long as it's an iron rod an inch thick and ten or twelve inches long and goes by the name of "rebar"), you poke four holes in the soil in one of the square planters, each hole six inches in from the edge of the planter and six inches from each neighbor. The depth of the hole is twice the length of the clove the hole will be receiving.

A teaspoon of bone meal goes into each hole. Bone meal, being mainly phosphorous, will help your babies get a good solid start in life.

You're ready to plant.

Each clove, flat end down, goes into its hole. The tip of the clove points up toward the deck of your fourth-floor neighbor so that when *he* falls through *his* deck (he's planting kiwis) he will be impaled. Should you decide to roast him, remember: ten cloves per pound, in a preheated 400° oven, fifteen minutes for each pound.

Do not press down on the tip of the clove once it is in the hole. Just set it securely, straight up, like a drill sergeant. You'll fill the hole with soil and you'll tamp the soil down with the garden tool, lightly, and you'll water again, lightly.

In the following weeks you will examine the planter boxes every day, wondering, after a month, why the garlic's not yet appeared. Have you made an error, such as planting the cloves tip down? Added too much bone meal? Too little? Have you given them too much water so that while they've been sleeping they've been rotting in their little soil shelter?

Then one morning, about four to six weeks after you planted your cloves, you see a green tip pushing up through the soil. The next day: another green tip, the first one now a spear. Within two to three weeks, depending on the internal clock borne by each of the four specific varieties, there will be more green spears.

Step back, get out of its way, and let nature take its course.

Weeds.

Because your bagged soil was almost certainly weed-free and because you're not likely to be victimized by wind-blown seeds, you'll have minor, if any, weeding problems. (Oh, but wait until you move to that big house with the big back yard.)

One or two of those four varieties you planted is almost certainly a Rocambole garlic.

In early spring, after the Rocambole's stalks are two to three feet tall, and the leaves are full and broad, a thick green stalk shoots up at the center of the plant. This is the famous, or infamous, scape.

In a week or two the scape will coil and then coil a second time. At the top of the stalk will be a sheathed collection of ten to forty tiny bulbils. If the scape is not cut the bulbils will flower. Because the flowers will

wither and turn brown, producing no pollen, they will not be fertilized and so will not produce garlic should you plant them. A caveat: there are exceptions.

These scapes compose the topic of unending argument. Some growers refuse to cut them, in order to gather the bulbils. Some say the garlic bulb in the ground will be smaller if the scape is not cut. Other growers, including myself, are convinced the scape sucks nutrients, or energy, from the bulb. I cut the scape almost as soon as it appears. So will you.

In Italy the scape, as well as the other greens (the stalks) and the white immature cloves, are used in soups and stews.

But *guarda*! In French: *en garde*. In English: *Watch it*!

Once the scape goes so far as to complete its circling routines, it will be stiff and woody. Inedible.

So cut it early, within days after it appears. You might want the early stalks and leaves for salads or stir-fries, or (see recipes) you might want to try to capture the sheathed bulbils and use them, as did the Mayan Indians, dried and crushed, the size and appearance of pepper flakes, for seasoning.

OK, so the cloves have been in the planters since late October. If at this point (early spring; say late March, early April) you were to dig up the clove it would look

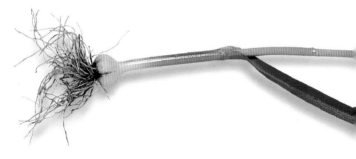

much like the clove you'd planted in October but a bit fatter, with hair roots ten or fifteen inches long. It would look as if it were straining at its skin.

You now want to help the clove do its garlic-thing.

Mix yourself a foliar spray composed of Maxicrop, a commercially available mix of minerals ($1/4$ teaspoon per gallon of water), and fish emulsion (two tablespoons to a gallon of water). Twice in the month of April (first day and last day) you'll spray the leaves, topsides and undersides. The second spraying can be applied as late as the first week in May.

In the next six weeks that clove will almost literally burst open.

By mid-May in most areas, like an adolescent crossing the line into maturity, the clove will have become a full bulb, size and shape and color and number of cloves decided by its own genetic dictates. The tips of the leaves are turning brown.

Whoa! Stop! No more watering!

The garlic needs this time to solidify, to dry down. Water now will have an effect on the tightness of the bulb, on its durability. It has reached its growth limits. Water now is like giving an adult growth hormones.

By early to mid June, depending on when and where the garlic was planted, and depending, too, on the variety, the bulb has reached its limits and the leaves, their aid no longer needed to supply nutrition, will begin to die. They turn yellow, then brown. When a half to two-thirds of the leaves are yellow-brown, in late June or early-to-mid-July (again, depending on where you live), the garlic is ready to be dug up. Because the soil is now dry and hard you'll need to work harder with your gardening tool.

You'll *dig* the garlic out of the soil, you won't *pull* it. Pulling the stalk can break it free of the bulb. At this stage, when the garlic still contains much moisture, breaking the stalks can lead to early rot.

Ideally, all sixteen cloves you planted survived. You have sixteen stalks, four of each of four varieties. Keep the varieties separated and identified.

Remove all the harvested garlic to the shade as soon as it's out of the planter box.

Hang the garlic, uncut, where it will be out of the sun and receive breezes. A pantry is OK if it's not too damp, and not too hot and dry. Remember: Keep the different varieties together and clearly labeled. You will want to know which variety you will be tasting (come dinner time, or breakfast!), which to keep, which to plant next year, which to replace.

You'll ignore the hanging beauties for two to three weeks, during which time the garlic will lose about 30 percent of its moisture. Then you'll trim the hair roots, cut the stalks about an inch above the head, and store your bounty in the pantry, in, ideally, clay pots with air holes, or in wicker baskets or other suitable containers.

During the summer you have several tastings. You consume garlic with a new passion. It is no longer someone else's product, it is yours. The word pioneer takes on new meaning. You might even buy a covered wagon and a team of mules. Or is it oxen?

Suddenly it's October again! Planting time!

But now, hooked—call it obsessed—you need more garlic, which means you need more space. Go west!

You go west, you buy that house with the big back yard.

Romanian Red

The alert aide at the nursery tells you about a fine book called *Growing Great Garlic* by Ron Engeland from Filaree Farm. You send for the book. You also order four new varieties of garlic from Filaree. With the fat healthy cloves you've saved from your own four varieties you will now have eight varieties, all of them different in shape and size and color and taste.

With so much yard you'll need not just advice, you'll need help.

You call an experienced gardener. He/she advises you not to plant directly into the backyard soil. The two of you will build planter boxes, larger than those on your previous deck, because such boxes will give you more control over more factors: the quality of the soil you'll need, the control of water

Achatami

A Brief Guide
for Growing Your Own
in Planter Boxes

1. **Soil:** well drained, medium to heavy, high content of green manure and humus if possible.

2. **Soil Prep:** Keep soil loose.

3. **Seed selection:** Choose a vigorous grower for your soil and climate; fattest, healthiest cloves.

4. **Planting:** depth of hole twice the length of the clove; cloves planted flat end down, tip up, four to six inches apart in row; plant two to three weeks before first frost; mulch if necessary or desired.

5. **Care:** weed; water or irrigate if necessary; snap off scape if it appears; try to keep free of water once leaves start browning.

6. **Harvest:** Dig up when half to three-quarters of leaves are brown, depending on variety; do not scar or injure bulb; do not leave in ground too long.

7. **Cleaning:** Garlic must be completely dry before cleaning; do not over-clean; leave as many outside skins as possible.

8. **Drying and Storage:** Dry entire bulb and stalk in a well-ventilated and airy location; spread on wire racks or tie stalks in small bunches of four to six, depending on size, and hang; dry two to three weeks.

9. **Storing:** for long term, 32° at 60 percent humidity; for kitchen use, hang in wire basket in cool shaded area; for very long storage, up to one year, clean and peel cloves and place in a jar containing $1/3$ apple vinegar and $2/3$ water and refrigerate.

With help from David Piedmonte
The Garlic Press Newsletter,
Spring/Summer 1995

during dry periods, the control of weeds, the control of underground predators such as gophers or moles. Again, you won't have to buy a lot of fancy expensive rototillers or cultivators or weed-whackers. You will need a few quality shovels (one of them flat-bladed and short-handled), a wheelbarrow, and a pair of gloves.

For now, you and your gardener build just two boxes. Next year you'll build two more. Maybe. After all, you still have to keep that nine-to-five job. You aren't that rich. And four boxes...whoa!...they mean work. Lots of it.

The yard, the gardener informs you, will comfortably hold six planter boxes and still leave you plenty of space for flowers and paths and a garden shed.

OK, a total of four next year, then six. After that: maybe you'll move to Gilroy.

The planter boxes on the deck of your apartment, as you had prepared them, have prepared you for what is to happen now. You and your helper build a box four feet wide and ten feet long, with half-inch mesh chicken wire stapled securely on the bottom. Impervious even to baby predators. Maybe.

A truck delivers carefully selected soil to your curb, dumps it, and you and your helper wheel it into the back yard and into the boxes. Fine exercise. No need for a membership in a gym anymore. Money saved.

After the boxes are full your helper covers the surface with newspaper, five or six pages thick, and soaks them with the hose. "Why the newspaper?" you ask. You are embarrassed when he tells you. It is so obvious, so simple. "We punch holes through the newspaper where we want to plant the cloves. The paper keeps the weed seeds underneath from germinating. Your hours of weeding will be reduced by 200 percent."

Using a measuring tape, your helper plots an imaginary grid on top of the newspaper. He punches a hole through the paper every six inches, enough holes to accept the cloves you now have from the garlic you grew and the new garlics you bought from Ron Engeland at Filaree Farms.

"What's that?" you ask your helper, who has just delivered a bale of straw. Straw, not hay, because it has far fewer enemy seeds.

"Mulch."

"What's mulch?"

"It goes on top of the newspaper. About six inches thick. It protects the garlic from marauding birds and it helps the soil stay moister longer. It will send up weeds but with just two boxes you won't have too much work. When you build more boxes next year, and more after that, you'll not use straw, you'll use…"

"Whoa! Let's stay with the two boxes for now."

The spaces in which you planted the different varieties are identified with plastic marking stakes. You've used waterproof ink, of course. But as a precaution, you've also drawn a little map. You've drawn the boxes, showing the labeled divisions. You might even have added the date of planting. You'll be surprised how one or another appears earlier or later, comes ready for harvest in early June or late June or even early July.

During the early autumn, if the rains delay, you keep the mulch and soil moist. This means you probably use sprinklers. An hour or two a day, every three days.

When it rains, you don't use the sprinklers, of course. But if there are long periods of no-rain you do turn on your sprinklers again, just to keep the mulch and soil moist.

Winter passes by. Spring comes. The garlic's knee high to a small elephant.

Summer. Oh oh, no rain. You keep the sprinklers working, the rhythm as before.

But the garlic has to dry down. That means not watering the last three weeks of the garlic's time in the soil.

Problems.

Because different garlics mature at different times, the drying down should vary. Given your situation—two boxes containing the eight different varieties, you can't easily dry-down one portion of a box and soak the other portions. Well, you have no choice but to dry them all down at the same time.

You've learned something.

Next year you will plant according to maturing-times, so one or more boxes will have early-maturing garlics and the other boxes will have the late-maturing.

Thus is the benefit of reading the labels to see when you'd planted the garlics and when, now, each goes dry. You'll store this information, of course, so that next year….

It's almost time to harvest.

People come from all over town to peer over your fence. "This is where that crazy person lives, the one who grows that weird garlic."

You're not dealing with little planter boxes on a

third-floor deck now, you have big boxes in a big yard. And you have that wire mesh on the floor of the boxes. You won't just be *picking* garlic now, you'll be *harvesting* it.

Which means you'll be using a shovel. Preferably a short-handled shovel with a wide, flat-edged blade.

Not a spade!

A spade has sharp tines that can pierce the wire floor with amazing ease and tear holes large enough for moles or gophers to invade. I've lost the entire contents of a box from which I'd harvested excellent garlic the year before. I'd used a spade, gone too deep, pried too energetically with the sharp tines, torn the wire. Result, unnoticed for nine months, one or more holes the width of two fingers, just the right size for a baby gopher to enter and, driven by family responsibilities, to haul plant after plant down through the hole(s) to brothers, sisters, cousins, aunts, uncles. And, of course, parents.

The box had been filled with 150 stalks on a Monday morning but by Wednesday, the box was empty.

You'll be less likely to tear the wire when you use the wide, flat-bladed shovel. Slip it into the soil at an angle, with the blade several inches from the stalk. This means the blade will find its way past and underneath the head, without cutting or scarring.

Angling the shovel and pushing the handle down will lift the blade, with the garlic head, or even heads, intact. Once the heads are free of soil, you can then pick up the stalks by the base and shake them free of excess dirt. Some growers hose off the dirt. I don't.

Promptly, immediately, instantaneously, protect the garlic from direct sunlight.

Using rope or string, nails or hooks, hang the stalks, roots, bulb and all, in the shade, exposed to the breezes. Let them all hang out for two to three weeks and then, with sharp pruning shears, cut the stalks an inch up from the bulbs and trim the hair roots.

Best for storing the free heads: mesh onion bags. A label fixed to each bag will identify the variety of garlic contained inside.

Done. It's time to eat. But remember: save the healthiest, fattest cloves for planting in the fall.

Four boxes next year? Six?

Are you tempted to buy a chunk of land in Gilroy?

If you do, don't give up your full-time job.

Best advice: Marry into one of the big Gilroy garlic ranch families. Inherit garlic. Pass it on.

4
Health

For those of you concerned about your health, remember: besides containing approximately two calories, one average-size clove of garlic also contains a variety of other nutrients not likely to be found in even your biggest, most expensive mineral-multi-vitamin pill: calcium, phosphorous, potassium, sodium, magnesium, aluminum, barium, and iron, along with thiamin, riboflavin, nicotinic acid, and Vitamin C.

And selenium.

And germanium.

One of the trace elements essential to good nutrition, selenium is important both because of its value as an antioxidant and for general protection against heart disease.

The work of Orville Levander of the USDA, using studies he'd made in China, recently resulted in a change in dietary standards issued by the Natural Research Council. Finding a debilitating heart condition known as Keshan disease to be linked to selenium-deficient diets, the NRC readjusted its recommended daily allotment to 70 mcg for men and 55 mcg for women.

Although it is generally believed that the soils of the Eastern U.S. are more deficient in selenium (due to historical glacial skimming of topsoil), the amount that remains is maximized by the consumption of raw garlic. If you live in the west, eat garlic; if you live in the heart of the heartland, eat garlic; but if you live in the east, eat lots of garlic.

Germanium.

Most of the research on this supplement has been done in Japan by Dr. Kazuniko Asai, who was aware of its high concentration in the earth's crust, and suspected its presence in plants. He concluded that germanium was present in highest concentration in plants used for medical purposes, including ginseng, aloe vera and garlic.

Germanium enhances the plant cells' ability to generate energy by raising the oxygen supply. Carrying this theory over into human research, Dr. Asai and Dr. Parris M. Kidd now think that germanium is capable of regulating blood pressure and reducing stress, especially the potential effects of pollutant stress. The protective action of cells in plants can be duplicated by human cells to protect the body.

Caution, as we pause here to consider the various garlic products available at almost every health food mall: raw garlic, garlic pills, garlic oil, garlic oil macerate, AGE (Aged Garlic Extract), all theoretically offering the benefits of the preceding trace minerals and other elements. Oil macerate, incidentally, is produced by blending chopped garlic with a common vegetable oil, such as soybean.

A bit of elementary garlic-chemistry has to be studied here. Work hard to understand this. There will be a quiz.

The active constituents in garlic are the *thioallyl* compounds, which comprise approximately one-half of one percent of all compounds in the clove by weight. The compound *alliin* is almost half of those compounds.

When garlic is crushed, its *alliin*, an amino acid, reacts with the enzyme *allinase*, which is also present. Normally, these two components are separated by a membrane but on physical disruption (smashing, cutting, biting, chewing), they break free of the membrane and join together.

All this in a microsecond.

As they join, or combine, the enzyme allinase converts the amino acid alliin to highly reactive sulfenic acids. These acids, in turn, spontaneously rearrange to form *allicin*, which, again spontaneously, rearranges to form a whole host of organo-sulphur compounds.

Note: Heat, such as in the cooking process, or in the dehydration process, can speed up and alter any or all of these rearrangements.

Of all the elements mentioned it is allicin that is almost universally considered responsible for the therapeutic properties with which garlic seems to be blessed.

Now a more simplified group of facts, relevant to the above, that enlightens us even more. There will be no quiz.

This is from a technical paper in the distinguished *Planta Med.* 57 (1991), pp. 263-270. Authors: Larry Lawson, S. Wood and B. Hughes.

> **Allicin** is believed primarily responsible for the anti-bacterial and anti-mutagenic effects of garlic.
>
> The allicin content of whole garlic averages about 0.4 percent of the total garlic weight. While isolated allicin is highly unstable in most environments, the allicin content of stored bulbs is fairly stable and seldom declines more than 10 percent maximum even after long storage. The allicin content of garlic can, however, vary five fold depending on the soil and climate where it was grown. In samples of foreign-grown garlic, the percentage of allicin ranged from 0.65 percent to 0.125 percent. In samples of U.S.-grown garlic from four states, the range was 0.458 percent to 0.23 percent. Soil appears to be the primary factor affecting allicin content. The allicin content of Elephant Garlic is **much lower** than that of true garlic. [Emphasis mine.] The allicin content of processed garlic products **was found to vary from 0.0 percent to about 75 percent** of the allicin found in whole garlic. [Emphasis mine.]

Meaning that *whole*, or *raw*, garlic, is not only far more likely to contain a greater amount of allicin but that that greater amount can be relied upon to be more consistent, more stable.

Trusting a summary of the cardiovascular effects of garlic as presented in 1993 by Larry D. Lawson, Ph.D., Murdock Healthcare, Springville, Utah, you should know what you are swallowing. Since 1975 there have been more than thirty human clinical trials conducted on the effects of garlic (garlic cloves, garlic powder, garlic tablets, garlic oil) on blood pressure and serum cholesterol. All of the studies in which patients consumed either garlic cloves or high allicin-yielding garlic powder pills, demonstrated significantly decreased blood cholesterol (6 to 29 percent) and triglyceride (8 to 34 percent) levels. In the eight studies measuring blood pressure there was an average decrease of 10 percent.

Lawson refers to a three-year study in India conducted by Dr. Arun Bordia. Of 432 people who had had prior heart attacks, half were given garlic-oil maceration (15 mg. undiluted/day) and half were given placebos. After three years, those taking the garlic-oil maceration had 35 percent fewer second heart attacks and 45 percent fewer deaths than the placebo group. Oil-maceration pills are rare in the U.S. but are quite common in Europe, where clinical studies have demonstrated that they do lower blood cholesterol and blood triglyceride levels. This type of mortality study, Lawson maintains, now needs to be conducted with garlic powder pills.

Considering the countless health fads being trumpeted these days, including food, and the undeniable, irrefutable, scientific evidence that proves the efficacy of an enormous complex of leaves and barks and grains and nectars, I'm tempted to ignore it all and just eat what I like and let the devil take my hindmost.

But I know I can't just eat what I like. Not if I want to live forever. And I, we, do want to live forever.

We must rely on a healthy diet so we don't get sick, so we can run a mile in nine minutes and then bench-press 1,000 pounds, so we can wear the trousers we wore when we graduated from high school or were twenty-one years old, whichever came first.

Does garlic raise or lower cholesterol?

Does garlic help counter different cancers?

Does garlic give us added energy?

Does garlic extend our life?

Will any research, performed by even ten Nobel winners, convince all of us all the time?

We pick and choose our experts, our research findings. Snake oil is cheap. But to get it you have to kill snakes, which I refuse to do.

Consider an article in the December, 1996 issue of *The American Journal of Clinical Nutrition* which refers to the study conducted by Manfred Steiner, MD/Ph.D., East Carolina University, *et al.* Described as "mid-size," the study involved fifty-six "moderately hypocholesterolemic" men who consumed AGE (Aged Garlic Extract).

The "major findings," meaning "results," according to the article:

> systolic blood pressures were 5.5 percent lower than the average pressure...

and:

> ...maximum reduction in total serum cholesterol of 6.1 percent or 7 percent in comparison with the average concentration during the placebo administration or baseline evaluation period, respectively.

This Steiner study was funded by the Irvine, California-based vitamin and mineral producer Nutrition International. The garlic for the study was supplied by California-based Wakunaga of America, which markets Kyolic brand AGE. Kyolic introduced its AGE in the United States in 1992 with a promotional campaign touting its cholesterol-lowering ability.

This is one of hundreds upon hundreds of research studies performed over the last ten years in the U.S., Europe, Asia, related to the healing powers of garlic. During these ten years science has been trying to prove, or disprove, the 6,000 years of anecdotal evidence referred to in the early pages of this text.

So far the provers seem to be victorious, despite the charges of the disprovers, such as the Wellness Clinic at the Berkeley campus of the University of California, which, in 1996, blasted the validity of all past and present testimonials to garlic's benefits. Garlic does nothing for the body, the Wellness Clinic newsletter informs us.

Remember the pleas of this and other such clinics, about five years ago, pleading with us to reduce our consumption of eggs to zero? Recently it has become not just acceptable to have eggs two or three times a week, but it might even be beneficial.

As this is being written (late 1996), major European and American news services are publicizing new garlic research by a team of British scientists. Garlic, the British scientists claim, does nothing for the body, it has no effect on cancer or cholesterol, contrary to what renowned scientists on three continents including Cornell have suggested.

No one in the news services or in the world of research focused attention on an important statement in those news reports (as well as those scientific documents) from Britain: the garlic used in the research was *powdered* garlic.

Powdered garlic is processed garlic.

Publications from Cornell and other universities, as well as clinics in Germany, India, and other countries, have stated for all (including the British research team) to see, that processed garlic has far less claim to therapeutic value than does raw garlic.

Writing in *The Garlic Press*, Fall 1991, five years before the British revelations, Howard Marks, a graduate student at Cornell, offers the British some American Revolutionary salvos.

In one scientific study (Saito et al., 1989, **J. Assoc. Off. Anal. Chem.** 72:917-920), researchers compared levels of allicin and alliin in processed garlic powders....they found that of the twenty garlic powders analyzed, eight contained no detectable level of allicin or alliin. Those products which did contain either of these two compounds had average levels of only 3.5 mg. alliin or allicin per **g** product. In addition, products which contained alliin did not contain allicin and vice versa. Raw garlic has been ana-lyzed and is found to contain approximately 30 mg alliin per **g** garlic (on a dry weight basis). There is almost a ten-fold difference between concentrations of precursor compounds found in raw garlic vs. processed garlic products.

Marks goes on to remind us that the severity of commercial processing techniques might destroy certain key garlic components.

...if allicin is present in a powdered garlic pro-duct, it may not be able to react with allinase when in the dried form, thus not being able to produce important therapeutic organo-sulphur compounds....

But now two alliumatic caveats.

Caveat Number One. The summary of an article in the American Botanical Council's *Botanical Series, 1991.* No. 311-Garlic.

Garlic, used as food and medicine throughout the world, has a history of use predating the written word. Garlic supplies are abundant, the herb is inexpensive, and is generally recognized as safe. Consequently garlic has been the subject of intensive scientific research over the past five decades, resulting in over 1,000 scientific publi-cations, which have shown antibacterial, antifun-gal, antitumor, hypoglycemic, hypolipidemic, and anti-atherosclerotic activity. These effects have been demonstrated in both animals and humans, though there is a need for more well-designed double-blind clinical trials to better determine therapeutic value, dosage levels, duration of treatments, and other parameters. Whatever the results of future research, garlic will likely remain as popular in the future as it has been for the past 5,000 years.

Caveat Number Two. You might be one of those few who are garlic-intolerant. Like those who are lac-tose-intolerant and who have to take precautions not to include the slightest amount of milk products in their diets, you might have to deny yourself the consumption of even the tiniest garlic clove or the weakest garlic tablet or pill. Though not common, several people have, after consuming garlic, demonstrated mild to severe dermatitis that is very similar to the dermatitis occurring after the consumption of other herbs or medications.

Now an important note: Do not haphazardly substitute garlic for any medication. Take into serious consideration your physician's advice regarding any decision to rely on garlic's therapeutic powers for any illness, real or imagined.

Herodotus and Tutankhamen and Homer knew nothing about allicin. But of course Herodotus and King Tut and Homer did not have the microscope. And they had no Ph.D. from Berkeley or Oxford.

I love garlic. I eat a lot of it, probably eight to ten cloves a day. I honor it as an herb which flavors the kind of food I like to eat, the food at which others might literally turn up their noses.

Should the 6,000 years of anecdotal history and past twenty years of scientific praise of the virtues of garlic prove eventually to be more false than true (which is highly improbable), I won't care and I don't much mind. I believe that legends, fables, folklore—the King James Bible, the Old Testament, the Koran, the I Ching, Fanny Hill—all have their roots in some event that occurred, some person who lived.

I'm thrilled to see and hear, over and over, the past and current stories about the powers of garlic. Herodotus and King Tut and Socrates and the ancient and contemporary Italians and Spaniards and Russians respected garlic as if it were as precious as rubies or diamonds. Personally, I'd like to have an equal amount of each.

When I taste garlic, honor it, sell it, give it away, meet other men and women from other countries, other cultures, who are as dedicated to the growing or the eating of garlic, or both, as I am, I feel those not just ancient but contemporary heroes reaching out to me. "Come on," they sing. "Taste this stuff I just pulled up out of the earth."

Garlic, to me, is not just healthy, it is essential.

That's not all, that's not even enough.

The growing of garlic, the eating of garlic, the talking and writing about garlic, is also great fun, which is better than a poke in the ear with a sharp stick.

5
Commerce

Between 1975 and 1994, the last year for which the U.S. Agriculture Department has records, annual U.S. garlic production almost quadrupled, shooting up from 140 million pounds to 493 million.

This year (1996) annual production will be about 800 million pounds. Of that, 600 million pounds will be grown in California alone, on more than 33,000 acres. Ninety percent of that amount will be grown in five counties: Fresno, Kern, Monterey, San Benito, Santa Clara.

All of these figures mean that each person in the U.S. will consume about two pounds of garlic this year: about a third of a clove a day. Far below several of the Asian countries where the annual average per person is forty to fifty pounds, about eight cloves a day.

The major portion of garlic grown in the U.S. is dehydrated for use in the production of catsup, mustard, sausage, pickles, and pet food. A smaller but still substantial portion goes into salts and powders. A comparatively small amount is used in the production of garlic tablets and pills and oil perles, most of it available in health food stores. Some 120 million pounds (about a sixth of the total national poundage) are sold fresh, meaning raw, in markets across the country.

An additional 100 million pounds of fresh garlic will be imported from other countries, such as Mexico, Argentina, Chile, Taiwan, Spain and, after fierce resistance from victimized American growers, from China.

China presents an interesting dilemma in the production and sale of garlic.

The *Production Yearbook* of the U.N.'s Food and Agriculture Organization gives a world garlic crop of 2,315,000 metric tons.

In 1985 the leading producer was China (it still is), with an estimated 550,000 metric tons, followed by

Spain, with 197,000 tons, South Korea, with 186,000, Thailand, with 180,000, Egypt with 166,000. Over the past 30 years garlic production has doubled in Spain, tripled in Egypt, Mexico, and Brazil, and quadrupled in the U.S, which means about 150 million metric tons.

Consider the following true-life scenario you never saw on television.

It is 1990. China, in desperate need of dollars, is preparing a trade strategy to flood the world markets with garlic.

1991. China exports three million pounds of raw garlic into the U.S.

1992. China exports seven million pounds of raw garlic into the U.S.

1993. China exports fifty-four million pounds (roughly equal to half the year's then total U.S. garlic production) of raw garlic into the U.S.

During these years California growers see their profits precipitously declining. They lose twenty percent of their peeled-garlic business alone.

1993. The national press reports that two freighters from China, each containing 2.2 million pounds of garlic (it turns out to be 3 ships with 4 million pounds each), are about to unload their cargo at Port Canaveral, Florida and Wilmington, Delaware. Selling price to American markets? Six cents a pound. China's cost of production? Twenty-five cents a pound. It must be inscrutable garlic.

Europe promptly limits imports from China to 20,000,000 pounds.

Mexico promptly imposes phytosanitary restrictions, which end all imports.

It so happens that Argentina, a major exporter of garlic, had suffered such heavy rains the previous December that its garlic had turned dark and unsalable. Result: no garlic to export.

In stepped Chile and Mexico with high-quality garlic offered at twice the price Argentina would have charged, had it had garlic to export.

When California growers lowered the standard price of their garlic to compete with Chile and Mexico, China promptly lowered its prices even more, thus winning easy access not just to European but to U.S. markets as well.

We're talking millions of pounds and millions and millions of dollars here.

Following appeals to Washington, Federal examiners promptly boarded Chinese ships at ports up and down the West Coast to examine cargoes. It should be no surprise to anyone, considering that China was trying to sell at well below production cost, that the International Trading Commission promptly slapped a 376.6 percent tariff on the Chinese imports. China was compelled to post a non-refundable bond, or cash deposit, at U.S. Customs.

All of this is what is often referred to as the vagaries of the stalk market.

As a featured speaker at the Hudson Valley Garlic Festival in 1993, Lyn Ciocca, a Vice President at Pacific Health Laboratories in New York, described a symposium she had attended. The symposium's topic: "Comparison of the U.S., European and Japanese Nutraceutical Health and Medical Rules."

At that symposium Dr. Stephen DeFelice (sponsor of the nonprofit Foundation for Innovation in Medicine) had defined a nutraceutical as "any substance considered a food, or part of a food, with medical or health benefits, including the prevention, cure, or treatment of a disease."

Such products, Dr. DeFelice had explained, include traditional foods, isolated nutrients, plants, dietary supplements (vitamins), genetically engineered designer foods, herbs, and processed foods such as cereals, soups and beverages.

And, according to Ms. Ciocca, garlic.

At the Hudson Valley Garlic Festival, Lyn Ciocca went on to compare the regulatory environment and the marketing support for garlic supplements in Germany, Japan, and the U.S..

The garlic-supplement market in Germany is currently worth $200 million dollars. (In Japan it is $150 million and in the U.S., $40 million.)

The best-selling pharmaceutical in Germany, a garlic capsule or tablet called Kwai, marketed by the Lictwer company, enjoys a 36 percent share of the market.

In Japan, the favored Kyoleopin and Leopin Five are marketed by the Wakunaga company, the developer of AGE (Aged Garlic Extract). These products alone account for 90 percent of the Japanese market.

The strength of Germany's garlic-supplement industry, one of the largest such markets in the world, is due to a system that allows health claims to be made for nutraceuticals. The German government believes sufficient scientific data exists to allow garlic supplements to claim success in preventing arteriosclerosis and lowering cholesterol.

In Japan, where garlic is regulated as a food, claims for health benefits are prohibited but components of garlic are included in the ingredient lists of AGE and other popular tonic products. These tonics are permitted to make general claims for the restoration of health.

In the United States it is illegal to make claims for garlic or garlic supplements. Though research in the U.S. has reported many positive conclusions, the opportunities for extensive research are limited. Most scientists in most research rely on federal funds and federal funding is very limited.

Pharmaceutical companies do not step in to supplement the funding. Because natural herbs do not offer certain returns on investments, it simply is not cost-effective for the industry to fund research to investigate the effectiveness of such substances. Medical research is very expensive and, given the restrictions of the federal health agencies, naturally occurring substances are very difficult to patent.

In both the production and consumption of garlic, as well as research into the benefits of garlic, the U.S. lags behind the rest of the world.

As awareness of garlic's medicinal powers grows among American consumers, and with more and more people relying on real food, food they can eat, or grow and eat, rather than supplements, it is almost inevitable that there will follow...next year, the year after, the year after that...a growing acceptance of the important therapeutic powers of raw garlic.

Over the last few years newspapers from the *New York Times* and the *Washington Post* to the local throwaways have touted the latest discoveries of garlic's curative powers. Kitchen and garden magazines, market newsletters, consumer bulletins, and investment advisers have been discovering and publicizing not just garlic in general but the many varieties of garlics, the new garlics offering not just health benefits but unique aesthetic and culinary pleasures.

You can eat and, at the same time, collect cultural bonus stamps.

It is almost impossible to find a garden catalogue that does not have an artist's palette of the *new* garlics in glorious color: Inchelium Red from the state of Washington or Creole Red from Louisiana or Spanish Roja or Russian Redstreak from near Leningrad or Xi'an from north China.

Inchelium Red

You are no longer *au courant* if you offer ordinary garlic to your family or your guests or your customers. *Roasted garlic* has become as much a part of *le vocabulaire de cuisine* as *pâté* or *crème brûlé* or *Visa*.

Like the garlic varieties themselves, garlic products vary in size, shape, color, composition. At the moment, until the growing momentum of raw garlic catches up, its alternatives have to be considered.

Example.

Among the available alternative products are garlic oil capsules, which are easy to take. But too often garlic capsules contain very small amounts of essential garlic.

Creole Red

Odor-controlled powder capsules release active ingredients only after the capsule is swallowed. Though the capsules contain 100 percent garlic powder it is impossible to know the amount of allicin created after digestion. Remember allicin ?

Partially odorful tablets, sold almost exclusively in Europe, contain alliin and allinase, which combine only after swallowing, so that the actual amount of allicin presented is both unknown and unpredictable.

AGE (aged garlic extract) consists of chopped garlic aged in alcohol for a long period, often a year or more. Apparently these extracts, which originated in Japan, lack garlic's important medically active ingredients. Research (see the prestigious British journal *The Lancet* of 15 January, 1990) suggests serious doubts about the product, stating unequivocally that such preparations are simply not effective.

Other garlic products, sold as food (garlic paste, garlic powder, granular dried garlic), are often dried with heat, which means that not only will they not contain the essential allicin but the effects, whatever they might be, diminish the longer the product is stored.

There is general agreement among scientists in Europe and the U.S. that, given the choice and the physical limitations, it is preferable to take, first, fresh garlic, then capsules or tablets rather than secondary garlic food products (powder, salt, etc.).

Dr. R. R. Sampson, of the Royal Infirmary in Edinburgh, wrote that the Infirmary's findings indicated that "... the garlic content in proprietary health food capsules is insufficient to alter platelet aggregation." Meaning: to improve health benefits.

Consider, if nothing else, the cost of capsule or tablet compared to the cost of raw garlic, which, incidentally, contains more allicin than your local French chef would want to shake a *sticque* at.

Each tablet will contain roughly 300 mg. dried garlic powder. So four tablets would be equivalent to a clove. A certain popular brand offers 100 tablets for ten dollars. That's ten cents each.

With four tablets equaling one clove, the worth of each clove is now forty cents.

Consider the average number of cloves to a bulb to be ten.

Ten cloves to a bulb (ten cloves times forty cents = four dollars a bulb) and six bulbs to a pound, means to Professor Einstein that this company is selling you garlic (powdered garlic! allicin-diminished or allicin-emptied garlic!) for almost twenty-five dollars a pound.

I sell my organic, special, exotic, gourmet, gorgeous, tasty, new, hand-planted, hand-cultured, lovingly caressed garlics for five to seven dollars a pound.

I am what German garlic lovers call a *dumbkopf*!

Russian Red Streak

Tomorrow I start dehydrating my garlic, grinding it under intense heat into powder, and pressing it into tablets, so I can go to the farmer's markets and pay less money for less space and peddle my garlic tablets to you. With my profits I'll buy a seat on that stalk exchange.

Xian

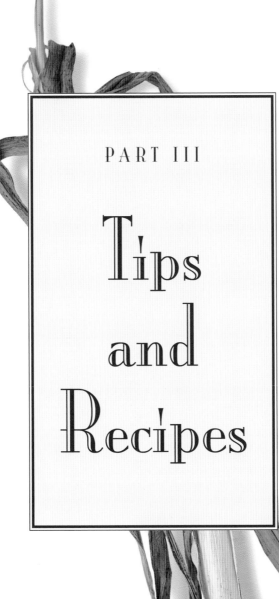

PART III

Tips
and
Recipes

6
General Tips

ROASTING GARLIC IN THE MICROWAVE

Garlic	Broth	Olive Oil	High Power	Low Power
1 head	1/4 cup	1 tablespoon	4 min. cooking	7 min. cooking
			5 min. standing	5 min. standing
2 heads	1/4 cup	2 tablespoons	5 min. cooking	10 min. cooking
			5-10 min. standing	5-10 min. standing
3 heads	1/2 cup	3 tablespoons	6-8 min. cooking	14 min. cooking
			10 min. standing	10 min. standing

To cook garlic heads in a microwave oven, trim stem ends of head to expose cloves. Use a 2-cup measure for one head, a 4-cup measure for more heads. Add chicken broth and oil to measure. Cover tightly with microwave plastic wrap and cook at 100 percent power. Remove heads from oven and let them stand, covered.

THE NEW YORK TIMES 2/12/92

My Preference: Roasting Garlic in the Oven

1. For a whole head of a single variety. Do not remove skins. Trim top of head (or bulb), exposing tips of all cloves. Place head, tip end up, in an oven-proof container (clay containers of all sizes and shapes now available). Sprinkle with olive oil. Light salting will help emphasize sweetness. Depending on size of head, or cloves, bake in preheated 375° oven for about an hour. When garlic is cool enough, tear off cloves and squeeze out garlic onto bread or unflavored crackers or a mellow, moderately firm cheese. If roasted uncovered, the creamy pulp is slightly dryer than that available in following techniques.

2. For heads, or cloves, of several varieties. Do not remove skins. Separate all cloves from head of a single variety (example: Spanish Roja) and snip off tips. Place cloves on strip of aluminum foil. Sprinkle with oil, lightly salt if desired. Wrap all oiled cloves in the foil, making a sealed envelope. With felt-tip pen, write name of variety on outside of foil. Prepare and identify another foil envelope of cloves from another variety.

Prepare as many different varieties as you wish. Keep foil envelopes in preheated 400° oven for 1 hour. Open foil envelopes, serve when cool enough, and compare the different tastes of the different varieties. This method is not as messy, leaves less tasty garlic behind, and offers clean, clear opportunities to compare the many different garlics available.

Any variety of garlic can be roasted, though the large heads (and cloves) are easier to manage. All varieties (depending on what is available and the flavors you like) are equally rich though some are more equal than others. My personal choices: California Late; Chesnok Red (from Shvelisi, Republic of Georgia); French Red, Leningrad, Mchadidzhvari (Republic of Georgia); Pitarelli (Czechoslovakia); Purple Glazer (Republic of Georgia); Yugoslavian Red; Siberian.

Refrigerate unused portions to use the next day or use part or entire portion for soups, sauces, stews.

One of the results of roasting garlic is the removal of sulphur, thus making much milder and sweeter the consequences in mouth and bowel and perspiration and relationships.

FRENCH RED
Hardneck Rocambole

Moderate-sized bulbs with 8 to 10 cloves colored rose to dark red. The flavor begins with a quick flash of heat, and remains quite strong. Stores longer than most Rocamboles. Also known as Hannan, the French region of its origin.

Garlic Roasted in Broth

Place desired amount of peeled cloves in a suitable casserole or pan. Cover cloves with chicken or beef broth. Place, uncovered, in a preheated 400° oven for 45 minutes. This adds a taste of extra dimension to the garlic but masks the specific garlic taste. Especially usable in sauces.

GARLIC OIL

Reported cases of botulism in Canada were traced to garlic butter that had been improperly stored. A minced garlic and oil preparation had been mixed with butter and spread on bread several days after its preparation. The mixture had not been refrigerated between its preparation and its use.

Garlic, a low-acid herb, can be stored by covering it with olive oil, but only after it has been acidified (by being soaked in vinegar for at least twelve hours). This vinegar bath prevents the growth of microorganisms which create the botulism toxin. The vinegar bath not only destroys botulism toxin but helps prevent browning of cloves. It also prolongs the quality of the garlic.

To be safe: Peel the garlic cloves and cover them with vinegar for twelve hours. Drain off the vinegar, which can then be used as garlic-flavored vinegar. Let the cloves dry and cover them with olive oil.

The oil can remain at room temperature and be used for two to three weeks before it turns rancid. Refrigerated, it can be used for three to four months. If refrigerated it should be removed and kept at room temperature long enough for the cold jelled oil to return to a fluid state before being used.

(Source: Dr. George York, University of California at Davis.)

MORE GARLIC HINTS

To remove garlic odor from hands: Rub hands with salt or lemon juice and rinse under cold water, then wash with soap.

To modify or eliminate garlic breath: Chew on fresh parsley (nature's breath mint) during and after meals; chew on a coffee bean; have a bowl of lime sherbet for dessert.

To help take the bite out of an especially hot garlic: Soak peeled cloves overnight in milk, which can later be used in appropriate dishes, such as sauces.

To more easily peel whole fresh cloves: Pour hot water over cloves for three or four seconds, then pull off skins with a sharp knife; soak cloves in icy water for about twenty minutes before peeling; put cloves into microwave oven for five to ten seconds before peeling; if only a few cloves are needed, use commercial tubular peeler now available, but be prepared for disappointment if cloves are fresh or only recently cured.

To press unpeeled cloves: Place clove base-down in a strong garlic press; after pressing, skins that are left behind can be easily removed; if cloves are too large, cut in half and place in garlic press cut side down; remove skins each time.

To make and store garlic butter: Mash garlic cloves and mix into soft butter; add chives and parsley and, if desired, salt lightly; form into logs; wrap in plastic; place in freezer bags; store in freezer; slice as needed.

Helpful hints: Fresh uncooked garlic is more pungent when puréed, crushed, chopped, or minced; for a milder garlic flavor, keep cloves whole or cut into large pieces; the flavor of garlic grows more delicate the longer it cooks; whole cloves cooked with roasts, stews or soups develop a sweet nut-like flavor; for pungent garlic flavor, add the garlic, freshly minced, to soups, stews, salads, or other dishes during last few minutes of preparation.

Have you ever seen one of those stop-action photographs of a sneeze? Out of the distorted face and open mouth: a spray of moisture, of droplets large and small, of mist.

I thought of such a photograph recently when I entered a kitchen where a chef I much admire was preparing a few garlic cloves for a sauce. Using the flat side of a heavy cleaver, he smashed the cloves.

The skins certainly did break free, as he had expected.

But had I taken a stop-action photograph with a fine-lensed camera at the moment the cleaver struck the garlic clove, the photograph would have displayed a dense spray of...of what? Of the various elements that help produce that allicin so highly acclaimed in health research, of the elements (mineral and vegetable) that define the specific garlic's taste. In other words, the age-old tradition of smashing the garlic clove defeats the purposes for which garlic is loved and used.

Don't do it. You wouldn't treat your wine or your cigar that way. Or your wife or husband. Or me.

Mayan Indian Garlic

You are about to be introduced to a use for garlic never described before in any anthropological or culinary appraisal of the herb and on which enterprising entrepreneurs will now invest.

Last year, Avisa, a young woman from Corales, New Mexico, worked with me in the field. Her mother, Barbara Rockwell, sent me two heads of a garlic that grows wild on her ranch in Placintas, New Mexico. The ranch is at 8,000 feet altitude.

I planted twelve cloves of Barbara's garlic last October.

Avisa's mother sent me in the same mail (collected in a knotted strip of silk hose), about a pound of the bulbils which grow at the top of the scape those wild garlics push up every year.

The bulbils, or seeds (inevitably sterile) on my top-set garlics here in California, are the size of pin-heads. Barbara Rockwell's New Mexican bulbils, dried by the New Mexican sun, are the size of chickpeas, almost the size of my thumbnail. They are so pungent that, even though securely wrapped in cardboard and brown paper, they created a minor revolution in the small post office in Occidental. The friendly superintendent called to beg me to please pick up my package. It was driving her colleagues out of the office.

She was correct. For a week after I removed the package from my car I remembered it every time I slid behind the steering wheel.

A month after the garlic's arrival I was visited by the courtly Ed Selyem, co-owner of Williams Selyem wines. Ed brought with him Mateo Granados, a former cook in various San Francisco restaurants. Granados now works for Ed and Gayle Selyem in their vineyard. As the two men stepped into my curing shed Mateo sniffed, looked around, picked up the bulbils still in their silk-hose wrapping, and put them close to his nose. "My grandfather," he said.

Mateo is a Mayan Indian, born in the village of Oxkutecal, in the Yucatan. His father and grandfather and great-grandfather had collected these bulbils in the Yucatan. Mateo described his grandparents and great-grandparents crushing such dried bulbils under a rolling pin. They collected the dust and particles in a bag. Whenever needed to flavor a dish, they were sprinkled like pepper flakes, sometimes lightly, sometimes heavily.

I have since crushed my New Mexican bulbils as Mateo's ancestors had. I have used them in stews and pasta sauces and in omelets. Depending on my generosity with the flakes, the food's pungency spurs me on through the day. In truly large amounts, it clears the sinuses.

I have planted other garlics that produce large bulbils (Asian Tempest for one). Late this spring I will not remove those scapes, but will let them remain to produce their bulbils.

I intend to market the product under the label Mateo's Miracle Mayan Flakes. Whoever buys this book automatically receives permission to use my recipe without payment.

7
Recipes

HOW AND WHY THESE RECIPES ARE HERE

Most of the people I know who are interested in cooking and eating have file drawers packed with recipes cut from magazines and newspapers, as well as those begged or borrowed or stolen from friends and family.

It was not difficult for me to know what I should do with my love—some would call it an obsession—for garlic. After all, my collection of fifty-five garlics came from seventeen different countries. I have traveled casually in six of them, passionately in three. I appealed to all of them.

I was curious about how the various cuisines of the various cultures represent their devotion to garlic. (Garlic is used in almost every cuisine in every culture. It is extremely important in some, moderately so in others, slightly relevant in six, scorned in two.) I started with one friend in San Francisco. A king of friends, Giovanni Leone, chef and owner of Buca Giovanni. He is now retired. From him I hopped to Paul Bertolli at Oliveto Restaurant in Oakland and then to Judy Rodgers at San Francisco's Zuni Cafe, and the race was on.

Chefs at restaurants in and out of the Bay Area where I've appreciated garlic dishes introduced me to chefs in other American cities. They in turn led me to garlic-loving chefs in Europe. Almost everyone to whom I appealed expressed delight at my venture and, after graciously contributing, guided me to someone else. I could not ignore those few friends whose home cooking I've enjoyed and who appreciate garlic almost as much as I do. Their recipes appear alongside those from the world's great chefs, where they belong.

My one regret is that my appeals to Asian chefs, here and abroad, went without response. That is unfortunate because more garlic is grown and consumed in China, Thailand, Vietnam, Korea, and Japan than in the rest of the world combined. But I tried. I do not want this absence to be misunderstood. Nor did I receive replies from French chefs. A French friend says that it was because my appeals were written in English.

With the receipt of over a hundred recipes—by mail, by fax, by Federal Express, by telegram—the problem of selection seemed unsolvable. The fraction represented here is, in my mind, or palate, the best of the best. They are presented, alphabetically, by restaurant or friend. The following index will help you to find specific dishes. Above all, enjoy!

RECIPE INDEX:

BUTTERS, SAUCES, DIPS, AND SEASONINGS

APPETIZERS AND SALADS

SOUPS AND STEWS

PASTAS

VEGETABLES AND SIDE DISHES

ENTRÉES

DESSERT

AKELLARE
Pedro Subijana, Chef

Capitol of the Spanish province of Gipuzkoa, in the Basque country, San Sebastian (or Donostia), on the Bay of Concha, is a center of Basque culture and folklore, with its own language, Euskera.

Akellare chef Pedro Subijana, who has championed Basque cuisine, has won, among other distinctions, the National Gastronomic Prize as Best Chef of 1979.

Throughout his professional career, Subijana has devoted himself to sharing his culinary experience. He has edited four books, has had a daily television program on which he demonstrates his recipes, and he has given many lectures and classes in Spanish, European, and American schools and universities. In his last visit to New York's Culinary Institute of America, Subijana was recognized as one of the ten best cooks in the world.

Subijana's oysters in cream of leek and fava bean vinaigrette and his poached egg yolk on truffle pasta and green asparagus, along with his traditional Basque dessert, foaming hot chocolate and chestnuts with sage, won Akellare Restaurant two stars from Michelin.

Creamed Garlic and Parsley Bream

Serves 4

Bream is a European freshwater fish, genus *Abramis*, with a flat body and silver scales. The closest North American equivalent is the sunfish, of the spiny-finned Centrarchidae family, which includes bluegill, black crappie, white crappie, and rock bass.

- 1 hot red chile pepper, such as a Fresno or a *huachinango,* chopped and seeded
- 1 jalapeño or *chilaca* chile pepper, chopped and seeded
- 3/4 cup extra virgin olive oil
- 1 head of garlic, cloves separated and peeled
- 2 bream or sunfish, each about 1 pound, cleaned, filleted, and with heads and skeletons reserved
- 1 carrot, chopped
- 1 leek, chopped
- 1 onion, chopped
- 1 bunch of parsley, chopped
- Salt and pepper

Place chile peppers in half of the olive oil and set aside. In a frying pan over low heat, slowly heat the peeled cloves of garlic in the remaining olive oil until garlic is golden, about 5 minutes. Set aside to cool.

Place fish heads and skeletons in a stockpot with the carrot, leek, and onion. Cover with water and bring to a boil. Boil for 15 minutes, remove from heat, stain, and set this stock aside. Put garlic and its cooking oil in a blender with parsley and 1/2 cup of the stock and blend until creamy. Pour through a fine-meshed sieve and set aside.

Season fish fillets with salt and pepper and cook lightly on a grill or a nonstick frying pan, leaving insides moist.

To serve, spoon 2 tablespoons of stock on each of four plates. Place a fillet on each plate and pour the pepper-saturated oil over each portion. Serve.

For this dish, I recommend a mild, moderately rich garlic such as Guatemalan Ikeda or California Early.

Garlic Anchovies with Parsley Sauce

Serves 4

Salt and white pepper

Juice of 2 freshly squeezed lemons

48 fresh anchovies, cleaned, with spines
    and tails removed, and butterflied

2 tablespoons red wine vinegar

Extra virgin olive oil

1 onion, finely chopped, for garnish

Chopped parsley, for garnish

2 slices red bell pepper

Parsley Sauce (recipe follows)

Garlic Sauce (recipe follows)

1 clove garlic, for garnish

Sprinkle a serving platter with salt and white pepper and the juice of $1/2$ of a lemon. Place the anchovies on the platter, then turn them over and season with salt and white pepper to taste. Sprinkle evenly with the remaining lemon juice and the vinegar.

Place anchovies on a hot grill for no more than a minute on each side, just long enough to lose the raw coloring within. Close each anchovy as if it were not boned and arrange on the platter in a fan shape. Brush the anchovies lightly with olive oil. Sprinkle with chopped onion and parsley and garnish with two slices of red pepper. Pour Parsley Sauce on the wide part of the fan. Pour Garlic Sauce over narrow part of fan. Garnish with a clove of garlic and serve.

PARSLEY SAUCE

Pinch of baking soda

1 bunch parsley, chopped

Salt and freshly ground black pepper

$1/2$ teaspoon cornstarch

Boil 1 quart of water with the baking soda, then add the parsley and boil for 30 seconds more. Drain parsley and place in a blender with two tablespoons of cold water. Blend at high speed until it forms a thick liquid. Season with salt and pepper to taste, then stir in the cornstarch.

GARLIC SAUCE

5 tablespoons vegetable oil

2 heads of garlic, cloves separated and peeled

Salt and freshly ground black pepper

Heat 3 tablespoons of the oil in a frying pan, then add the garlic cloves. Simmer on medium heat for 10 minutes, stirring. Drain garlic cloves, place in a blender, and blend at high speed until a purée forms. Add the remaining 2 tablespoons of oil and salt and pepper to taste, then blend again until fully combined.

For this dish, I recommend the same garlics as for the preceding dish: Guatemalan Ikeda or California Early.

GUATEMALAN IKEDA
Softneck Silverskin

Seed from Janet and Margaret Ikeda, from village of Aguacatan in Guatemalan province of Huehuetenango. Small to moderate bulbs, with small porcelain-skinned cloves. Very tall thin stalks (to 3 or 4 feet) with long thin fernlike leaves. Produces a very small scape, like a Rocambole. Mild, nutty flavor.

ARNAUD'S
Archie and Jane Casbarian, Proprietors

Arnaud's, the grande dame of French Quarter restaurants in New Orleans, was established in 1918 by Count Arnaud Cazenave, a French-born bon vivant with a talent for combining Creole cuisine, fine wines, and an elegant ambiance.

When Arnaud died in 1948, his daughter Germaine, a socialite who ruled over more Mardi Gras balls than anyone else in history, transferred her flair for the dramatic to the restaurant.

In 1978, Germaine passed the restaurant to Egyptian-born Archie Casbarian, the general manager of a French Quarter hotel.

Casbarian, after poring over old documents and menus and interviewing patrons of the original restaurant, set about renovating the restaurant. It features two bars, dining rooms on two floors, and a Mardi Gras museum, where Germaine Arnaud's Carnival costumes are showcased.

The cuisine is based on the re-creation of the original Arnaud's menu. Featured among the many dishes patrons of the old restaurant remembered fondly are Shrimp Arnaud, Trout Meunière, Filet Mignon Charlemond, Bread Pudding, and Crème Brûlée.

At Arnaud's, as a reminder of Provence, garlic butter is used for a variety of dishes, including Crab Claws Provençale, Frog Legs Provençale, Shrimp Clemenceau, and Crabmeat Monaco.

Garlic Butter

1 3/4 cups (3 1/4 sticks) butter, softened

1 cup chopped parsley

1/4 cup Herbsaint liqueur
(Pernoud can be substituted)

1/8 cup (about 6 cloves) chopped garlic

Salt and freshly ground black pepper

Place butter in a mixing bowl. Add parsley, liqueur, and garlic. Mix at low speed with a hand-held mixer until well blended. Season to taste with salt and pepper.

For garlic butter served with seafood, I recommend Louisiana's own prize-winning Creole Red garlic.

Crabmeat Monaco

Serves 6 as an appetizer

1/2 cup Garlic Butter

1 1/2 cups finely sliced mushrooms
(about 3/4 pound)

1/2 cup chopped scallions

1/2 cup chopped shallots

1/8 cup chopped garlic

1/2 cup diced tomato

1/4 cup tomato purée

3 whole bay leaves

2 pinches whole thyme leaves

2 1/2 pounds lump crabmeat,
picked clean and rinsed

3/4 cup Glassage (optional, recipe follows)

3 lemon halves, for garnish

Parsley sprigs, for garnish

Preheat the broiler. Melt the garlic butter in a saucepan over high heat. Add mushrooms, scallions, shallots, and garlic, and sauté for 3 minutes. Add diced tomato, tomato purée, bay leaves, and thyme. Bring mixture to a boil for 3 minutes. Lower heat and simmer for 5 minutes. Add crabmeat and bring back to a boil for 3 minutes to heat through. Stir gently to avoid breaking up the crabmeat.

Divide mixture evenly into 6 ramekins. Cover each with approximately 2 tablespoons Glassage. Brown quickly under the broiler for about 10 seconds. Place each ramekin on a dinner plate, garnish with half a lemon and parsley and serve.

Glassage

Makes 1 cup

This recipe calls for hollandaise and fish stock, recipes for which can be found in any good "basics" cookbooks, or they can be bought commercially.

Glassage is a traditional French glaze that imparts flavor and eye appeal to many dishes.

$^1/_4$ cup plus 2 tablespoons fish velouté (thick stock)

$^1/_2$ cup hollandaise sauce

$^1/_8$ cup heavy cream

In a mixing bowl, add velouté to hollandaise, using a mixer at low speed. In a separate container, whip cream until it thickens but does not yet make peaks. Stir cream into velouté-hollandaise mixture.

ADDITIONAL VARIETIES

ACHATAMI
Hardneck Rocambole

Heads are moderate to large in size, and often tangled in appearance. Quite hot at first, rapidly fading to a mild flavor that is rich and earthy. Difficult to peel.

CHESNOK RED
Hardneck Purple Stripe

Seed from Filaree Farm. From Shvelisi, Republic of Georgia. Large, nicely colored bulbs with many rose to red cloves. Good aroma and rich, lingering flavor. Exceptional for baking.

FRENCH WHITE
Softneck Artichoke

From a farmer's market near Stuttgart, Germany, by way of Egmont Tripp's Sunshine Farm in Cloverdale, California. Medium-to-large bulbs with 10 to 12 rounded cloves. Longer-storing than most Artichokes. Flavor has a sharp bite.

GABI'S PURPLE
Hardneck Purple Stripe

Egmont Tripp found the garlic in Germany; it is originally from Mexico. Substantial, bulky garlic heads with medium-sized blue or purple cloves. Heat lingers on and on.

IDIDARED
Hardneck Porcelain

Seed from Filaree Farm. From Republic of Georgia. Large bulbs with red-tinted wrappers and 8 to 10 large cloves with red-tinted skins. Strong flavor when raw, with warm pleasant aftertaste. A good salsa garlic or salad warmer.

not pictured

ELEPHANT
Allium ampeloprasum

Not a garlic, but a member of the leek family. Occasionally produces a single golf-ball-sized bulb, but more often yields a 4-to-6 clove bulb that can weigh a pound or more.

BARCELONA
Thomas Stegmaier, Executive Chef

Devotion to the culinary profession comes quite naturally to Thomas Stegmaier, whose mother was a cook in London and whose grandfather was a pastry chef in Germany. Stegmaier was born in Germany, and trained in hotels and restaurants in Switzerland and Germany. He received a diploma in 1982 from the Deutscher Hotel und Gastattenverband *in West Germany. From 1985 to 1992, he served as Executive Chef at Hotel La Bobadilla, in Seville, acquiring and holding a three-star rating from Michelin.*

After arriving in the U.S. in 1994, he served as Executive Chef at Costa de Sol in Hartford, Connecticut. In 1996, Stegmaier and his wife and daughter moved to California, where he founded Barcelona, in San Francisco.

DUGANSKIJ
Hardneck Purple Stripe (marbled group)

Seed from Filaree Farm. Originally from the Czech Republic. Plants short and stocky. Nice size bulbs averaging 6 brown cloves with slight purple blush. Taste is strong, earthy, heat dissipating fast. One of best-storing strains.

White Almond–Garlic Soup with Grapes

Serves 4 to 6

8 ounces blanched almonds, ground

3 slices white bread without crust, chopped

10 cloves garlic, peeled

6 cups milk

2 teaspoons sherry vinegar

2 cups extra virgin olive oil

Salt and freshly ground black pepper to taste

36 white seedless grapes, sliced in half, for garnish

Mix almonds, bread, garlic, milk, and vinegar in a blender at medium speed until well-blended. Switch blender to high speed and slowly add olive oil until the mixture is smooth. If the mixture tastes too strongly of either garlic or vinegar, add a small amount of water. Add salt and pepper to taste. Chill soup for several hours. Serve in bowls with grape halves.

For this recipe, I recommend a hot garlic: California Late, Asian Tempest, or German Red. For those who like moderately hot garlic, try the mellower Duganskij from the Czech Republic.

Sweet Garlic Sauce
for Meat

Makes 6 to 8 cups

Milk is used in some cuisines to cut the strength of garlic. Sweet grapes, cantaloupe balls, or bite-sized chunks of apples also offset the heat of both peppers and garlic. This sauce keeps up to two weeks in the refrigerator.

4 cups milk

3 3/4 cups sugar

12 large garlic cloves, peeled

In a large bowl, mix milk, 1 1/4 cups of the sugar and the garlic cloves. Cover and chill for 24 hours. Remove garlic cloves from milk and set aside. In a medium saucepan, mix half of the milk with 2 cups sugar and bring to a boil over medium heat. Add reserved garlic cloves and cook until garlic is tender, about 15 minutes. Remove garlic cloves from milk, discarding the milk. In a small skillet over low heat, melt the remaing 1/2 cup of the sugar, stirring constantly, until it is a rich, golden color, about 5 minutes. Add the cooked garlic cloves and cook lightly for 5 minutes, continuing to stir. Serve warm over meat of your choice.

I recommend a strong garlic that starts out sweet and only gets sweeter, such as Arden or Mazatlán.

MAZATLÁN
Hardneck Rocambole

Seed from Janice Dent, found in Mazatlán market. Stalk looks distorted, with fernlike projections. Size of bulbs unpredictable, can be very small or quite large. Cloves very small at first planting in my soil. Very hot but the rich taste shines through.

Country Chicken Breast
in Port Wine Sauce

Serves 10

5 whole chickens

10 1/2 ounces chopped carrots
   (3–4 average carrots)

5 1/2 ounces chopped celery
   (2–3 average stalks)

3 onions, chopped

1 handful fresh thyme (leaves and stems)

1 sprig rosemary

1 head garlic, cloves separated, peeled,
   and chopped into small pieces

5 tomatoes, chopped

5 tablespoons olive oil

1 bottle red wine plus 6 cups red port wine

Salt and freshly ground black pepper
   to taste

Remove all chicken bones and cut into small pieces. Bake in a 400° oven until brown, 30 to 40 minutes.

Place all boned meat, except breasts, into a stockpot; cover with water. Boil for 1 hour, cool, strain, and set aside. In a very large saucepan, sauté carrots, celery, onions, thyme, rosemary, garlic, and tomatoes in 2 tablespoons of olive oil until heated through, about 5 minutes. Add roasted bones and the bottle of red wine and cook over medium heat until it begins to stick to the pan, about 10 minutes. Add 2 quarts of chicken broth and cook slowly until reduced by half. Let the mixture cool slightly, then strain through cheesecloth. Set aside.

Place the 6 cups of port in a large saucepan over medium heat; simmer until reduced by half, about 10 minutes. Add strained red wine reduction, salt and pepper to taste, and set aside.

Preheat oven to 400°. Season chicken breasts with salt and pepper. In a large ovenproof skillet over medium heat, sauté chicken breasts in the remaining oil until browned on both sides; then bake for 10 minutes. Place chicken on a platter, cover with sauce, and serve.

For this earthy peasant dish, I recommend an earthy garlic—Armenian.

LA VIEILLE MAISON
Robert Charles

La Vieille Maison, opened in the mid seventies, was the world's first garlic-theme restaurant. The owner and chef, Robert Charles, a legendary restaurateur, had had a one-star restaurant in the south of France before he went to San Francisco. He served only lamb dishes. He, the food, and the restaurant became a mecca for knowledgeable and appreciative diners. From San Francisco, Charles went to San Rafael, where he opened Maurice et Charles, again a congregation site for people searching for fine food. After San Rafael, Charles moved to Truckee, in northern California to establish La Vielle Maison, which was legendary even before it opened. Devotees traveled from all parts of the state and nation to dine in Truckee at Charles' restaurant. The following soup was named for the man who helped initiate the very first—and still the most famous—garlic festival in Gilroy, California. In return, Harris included the recipe in Addison-Wesley's 1979 revised edition of The Book of Garlic. *"This is a rich creamy soup," Harris says. "A little like the classic* Soup a l'oignon.*"*

Soup Lloyd J. Harris

Serves 4 to 6

4 to 6 cloves garlic, minced

6 large onions, finely chopped

$1/2$ cup butter

1 teaspoon flour

Pinch of thyme

Salt and freshly ground black pepper to taste

2 cups dry white wine

4 cups chicken stock

4 to 6 eggs

6 ounces grated Swiss cheese

$3/4$ cup heavy cream, whipped

Preheat oven to 350°. In a large saucepan over low heat, sauté garlic and onions in butter until they begin to brown. Add flour and stir until well-coated. Add thyme, wine, salt and pepper to taste. Bring to a boil and continue cooking for 30 minutes. Add stock and bring to a boil. Place in an 3-quart ovenproof casserole. Place casserole in the oven and bake for 1 hour.

Divide soup into small ovenproof casserole or soup bowls.

Beat an egg into each serving of soup. Sprinkle grated cheese on top. Bake in the 350° oven for 10 minutes. When ready to serve, dollop 2 tablespoons cream onto each serving.

For this dish, I suggest using a sharp, but rich and earthy garlic, such as Russian Red Toch.

Russian Red Toch

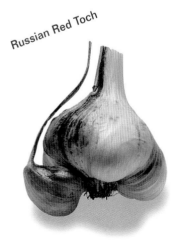

ENZO'S
Miki Zivkovic, Executive Chef

Miki Zivkovic was born in Belgrade, Serbia. His parents, children of World War II, "…lost all their possessions except love." As he grew up, Miki spent hours at the stove every day with his mother. He owes his love of cooking to her. As a young man, he enrolled at the Culinary Academy of Belgrade and after graduation, he worked in several Belgrade restaurants. The Executive Chef at the Hyatt Regency offered Zivkovic the position as chef de partie, *and soon after, as reward for his accomplishments, Miki was offered the chance to go to the United States to be a chef at the Hyatt Regency Hotel in Sacramento, California. He needed more challenge to his creative instincts, so he moved to San Francisco to work as a chef at Albona, one of two Istrian restaurants in the United States (Istria is a Croatian/Slovenian peninsula on the Adriatic). Two and a half years later, he got the opportunity to work with the internationally respected master chef, Alain Rondelli. In 1995 Enzo Polacco, who had met Zivkovic and appreciated his talents, invited him to be Executive Chef at his new Oakland restaurant. Here, Zivkovic says, at Enzo's, he is free to "…create dishes that are as much a reflection of my own vision as they are of the cuisine that influenced them."*

Stuffed Portobello Mushrooms

Serves 10

The completed composition of the mushroom is like an edible sculpture—the brioche is cut into cylinders that form the mushrooms' "stems," and the portobellos serve as the caps. You can, if you wish, buy brioche at your local bakery, instead of making your own.

PORTOBELLO CAPS

**10 portobello mushroom caps
(reserve stems for filling)**

10 tablespoons canola oil

**Salt and freshly ground black pepper
to taste**

Preheat oven to 350°. In a skillet over medium heat, sauté caps in the oil for 1 minute. Season with salt and pepper. Place caps on a baking sheet and bake until tender but still firm, 10 to 12 minutes. Set aside.

BRIOCHE STEMS

6 cups all-purpose flour

$1/2$ cup plus 2 tablespoons granulated sugar

$4\,1/2$ teaspoons salt

$1\,1/2$ ounces active dry yeast

10 eggs

**1 cup plus 2 tablespoons cold unsalted
butter, diced**

6 tablespoons unsalted butter, melted

6 cloves garlic

Place flour, sugar, and salt in large bowl. Add yeast and mix. Add eggs and butter and mix. Refrigerate overnight. The next day, remove the dough from the refrigerator and let stand 1 hour at room temperature. Preheat oven to 350°. Spray 10 small brioche molds with nonstick cooking spray. Divide risen dough into 10 pieces and place in molds. Bake until golden brown, approximately 35 minutes. Remove from oven and let cool.

Increase oven temperature to 400°. Press garlic into the melted butter and warm, on low heat, 2 minutes. Cut cooled brioche into cylinder shapes 2 x 2 1/2 inches. Brush cylinders with garlic butter and place in oven until golden (approximately 10 minutes). Scoop out the center of each brioche and set aside.

For the brioche, use a moderately hot garlic, spicy at first, with good but not strong aroma, such as Yugoslavian Red or Persian Star from Samarkand, Uzbekistan.

FILLING

2 onions, finely chopped

1 to 2 tablespoons olive oil

10 portobello mushroom stems, diced

1 tablespoon freshly grated Parmesan cheese

2 cloves garlic, finely chopped

Place onions and oil in a skillet over medium heat to carmelize, about 30 minutes, while frequently stirring. When onions are browned and syrupy, transfer, along with any bits clinging to skillet, to a bowl. Add mushroom stems, cheese, and garlic and mix well.

For this filling, I recommend a garlic with a hot, rich, lingering flavor—Russian Sanctuary.

SAUCE

5 onions, julienned

6 cups merlot wine

2 tablespoons unsalted butter

6 bay leaves

2 tablespoons freshly ground black pepper

1 teaspoon cumin

Place the ingredients in a sauté pan over medium heat and simmer until sauce thickens, about 10 minutes. Remove bay leaves and lower heat; keep sauce warm until ready to use.

To assemble, preheat oven to 400°. Stuff each scooped-out brioche with filling. Place the stuffed brioche in a baking pan with the baked mushroom caps. Roast in oven 5 to 6 minutes.

To serve, spoon equal amounts of sauce onto 10 serving plates. Place roasted, stuffed brioche in the middle of each plate, upright in the sauce, so that it stands like the stem of a mushroom. Place one cap on top of each brioche and serve.

RUSSIAN SANCTUARY
Hardneck Rocambole

Formerly identified as Light Tan. Reputedly from a Russian sailor who jumped ship in Vancouver many years ago. The garlic was offered in gratitude to the man who offered him asylum and the seed found its way to Helen Schultz in Washington. She offered it to me. It is now grown and sold at Kurt's Produce in Monroe, Washington. Stalks and leaves tall and strong. Large bulbs with 8 to 10 large, tan-skinned cloves. Hot, rich, lingering flavor.

MARGOT FANGER

Margot Fanger is a Californian living abroad in Boston. Among her ongoing careers, she is a mental health clinician at the Harvard Community Health Plan; a lecturer on psychiatry at Cambridge Hospital, Harvard Medical School; a master programmer in neurolinguistic programming; a certified hypnotist; and coauthor, with Steven Friedman, of the book Expanding Therapeutic Possibilities: Getting Results in Brief Therapy *(Lexington Books/Macmillan, 1991). Margot has been cooking hypnotic and therapeutic meals for her family, and occasionally for me, for 55 years, including this tasty pesto.*

Cilantro Pesto

Makes 1 cup

1 to 2 bunches fresh cilantro

4 to 8 (or more) cloves garlic,
   well-chopped

$1/2$ cup extra virgin olive oil
   (or enough to make a paste)

Clean cilantro well, shake and pat dry, and pick off leaves. In a food processor, chop garlic well. Add cilantro leaves and process again. Add enough oil to make a paste. The pesto can be packed into an ice cube tray or plastic container for freezing. Use as your secret agent for pasta sauces, casseroles, soups, and other dishes calling for pesto, defrosted only as needed so that the flavor remains intact.

The recommended garlic is the sweet and mild Arden.

ARDEN
Softneck Silverskin

From Nyak, New York, via Sherry Arden; originated in Dusgurov in the Ukraine. Medium bulbs with 12 to 20 small, tight, off-white cloves. Flavor is sweet and mild.

HOSTINEC U KALICHA
(AT THE CHALICE)
Pavel and Tomas Topfer, Owners

There are many restaurants in Prague that, eighty years ago, had been frequented by Jaroslav Hasek, the author of the Good Soldier Svejk, *and the painter Joseph Lada, who gave the famous Svejk his face and figure. But the location of Svejk's arrest and of the meeting "at six in the evening after the war," was Hostinec U Kalicha.*

Of Prague's innumerable notable places of interest, the restaurant U Kalicha on Na Bojisti Street (a few minutes' walk from Wenceslas Square and a dozen steps from the I. P. Pavlov Underground Station) is exceedingly attractive.

It was here that the "Good Soldier Svejk" entered the history of World War I. On June 29, 1914, the plainclothes policeman Brettschneider arrested Josef Svejk, a modest hero of the turbulent times, and arrested, in the evening of the same day, the pub owner Palivec.

The current owners of this restaurant, the brothers Topfer, are proud of Hasek and Svejk, and proud as well of Czech cuisine. "Czech cuisine," the Topfers tell me, "is heavy, fat, unhealthy, but very nice."

To illustrate the power of garlic in the Czech culture, Pavel and Tomas Topfer have offered me a traditional Czech saying: "The houses of those who eat onions never need to be visited by a doctor; the houses of those who eat garlic are never visited by anybody."

Potato Pancakes

Serves 4 to 6

6 large or 8 small potatoes

1 egg

1 tablespoon milk or cream

2 to 3 tablespoons flour

Salt and freshly ground black pepper
to taste

1 teaspoon marjoram

2 cloves garlic (or more if preferred),
pressed or minced

$1/2$ pound ham, diced (optional)

1 to 3 tablespoons oil

Grate the potatoes coarsely into a medium-sized bowl. Beat the egg and add to potatoes. Add milk and stir for 1 minute. Add salt and pepper to taste, and marjoram. Add the garlic and, if desired, the ham. Stir again for 1 to 2 minutes. Shape mixture into patties $1/4$ to $1/3$-inch thick. In a heavy iron skillet, heat oil over medium heat. Fry patties until brown and crisp, about 5 minutes per side. (**Note**: As a side dish, served with either baked meats or poultry, the pancakes can be as small as 2 inches in diameter. As an entrée, they can be as large as 8 inches.)

For this dish, I recommend either of the two Czech garlics, the Duganskij or the Monshanskij.

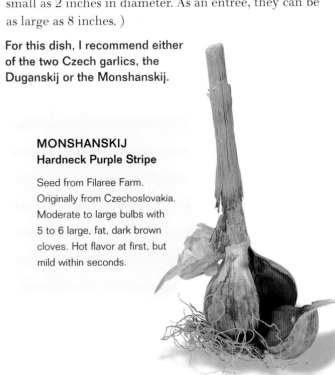

MONSHANSKIJ
Hardneck Purple Stripe

Seed from Filaree Farm.
Originally from Czechoslovakia.
Moderate to large bulbs with
5 to 6 large, fat, dark brown
cloves. Hot flavor at first, but
mild within seconds.

JOHNNY GARLIC'S
Guy Fieri and Steven Gruber, Owners

Steve Gruber, originally from Pennsylvania, received a B.S. in hotel and restaurant management from Penn State. He has had extensive experience in the food and beverage industry and has been Chef and General Manager with Restaurant Enterprise Group.

Guy Fieri is from northern California. He has worked in various aspects of the restaurant industry, from flambé chef to prep cook. After studying abroad, he received his degree in hotel and restaurant administration from the University of Nevada, Las Vegas, and became senior manager for Stouffer Restaurants.

Gruber is Head Chef at Johnny Garlic's in Santa Rosa, California, and Fieri is directly in charge of service. Since the restaurant opened in mid-autumn, 1996, there has been standing room only, day and night, seven days a week.

CHINESE SATIVUM
Softneck Artichoke

Fairly large bulb with 15 to 20 fat, medium-sized cloves curved up tightly against a central core. Color ranges from rose blush to red stripes. Long-lasting bite, but can be very hot one season and moderate the next.

Penne with Asparagus and Garlic Pesto

Serves 2

2 tablespoons olive oil

1 teaspoon chopped garlic (about 2 cloves)

1 teaspoon chopped shallots
    (about 2 shallots)

$1/2$ cup whole button mushrooms
    (4 to 6 mushrooms)

$1/2$ ounce sundried tomatoes, julienned
    (about 1 tablespoon)

4 to 6 average-sized asparagus spears,
    blanched and chopped

9 ounces penne pasta

$1/2$ cup garlic pesto (use the following
    recipe, Margot Fanger's Cilantro Pesto
    on page 83, or your favorite)

1 ounce Parmesan cheese, freshly grated

Salt and freshly ground black pepper to taste

1 plum tomato, diced, for garnish

1 small can sliced black olives, drained,
    for garnish

Heat oil in a sauté pan over medium heat. Add garlic and shallots and sauté until translucent, about 4 to 5 minutes. Add mushrooms, tomatoes, and asparagus and sauté until al dente, about 10 minutes. Blanch pasta in boiling water and add to sauté pan. Remove the pan from the heat and add pesto, which will be warmed by the pasta and vegetables. This prevents pesto from browning. Toss half of the Parmesan cheese into pan and stir to lighten sauce. Season with salt and pepper. Place on warm serving plates, and garnish with remaining Parmesan cheese, diced tomatoes, and olives.

I recommend for this dish a hot garlic, such as the California Late or Chinese Sativium.

GARLIC PESTO

Makes 2 cups

8 cloves garlic, minced

1 bunch fresh parsley, rinsed

4 ounces pine nuts

Dash of extra virgin olive oil

8 ounces cream cheese,
    at room temperature

1 bunch fresh basil, stems removed

Put garlic, parsley, pine nuts, olive oil, cream cheese, and basil in a blender or food processor and blend to a creamy consistency. This pesto can be stored, covered, in the refrigerator for 1 week.

For this pesto, Spanish Roja is best.

XIAN
Hardneck Purple Stripe

Seed from Filaree Farm and an unknown lady in San Francisco's Chinatown. A very rare garlic from northeastern China. Tall, thick stalks and wide heavy leaves. Very large bulb with thumb-sized cloves covered with purple-red, almost black skin. Taste is not too hot but very rich. One of my favorite garlics.

Caramelized Garlic Vegetable Lasagna

Serves 6 to 8

2 pounds lasagna pasta, blanched

1 cup olive oil

1 to 3 heads garlic, cloves peeled

1 teaspoon granulated sugar

2 quarts tomato sauce

2 pounds ricotta cheese

$1^1/_2$ pounds mozzarella cheese, grated

1 cup freshly grated Parmesan cheese

About 1 pound seasonal vegetables,
   sliced thinly and blanched

Preheat the oven to 350°. Boil about 2 quarts water in a stockpot and cook pasta until al dente, about 12 minutes (it will continue to cook while in oven). In a saucepan, simmer oil, garlic, and sugar on medium heat until garlic caramelizes, making it very sweet. Mix this soft garlic into the tomato sauce in a bowl, keeping about 12 cloves to garnish the finished dish. Mix ricotta, 1 pound of the grated mozzarella, and the Parmesan together. Layer the sauce first to coat bottom of a large lasagna pan, then pasta, $1/_2$ of the cheese mixture, and the vegetables. Top this with a layer of pasta, sauce, reserved mozzarella, and finally, the caramelized garlic cloves. Bake in the oven for 30 to 45 minutes, covered. Bake, uncovered, until cheese browns (about 10 more minutes). Cool 10 minutes. Serve, garnished with reserved garlic cloves.

With this abundance of cheese, vegetables, and pasta, a heavy, moderately hot, but very rich garlic is needed, such as Russian Red Toch, or Armenian, or Xian.

MICHELE ANNA JORDAN

Michele Jordan worked for years as a professional chef but in 1991, "shortly after making 2,000 miniature smoked-chicken tamales for the Sonoma County Wine Auction, I said enough is enough and embarked on a career as a full-time writer."

In the spring of 1995, Jordan was instrumental in creating a formal sister relationship between Sonoma County and Provence, France, "... two parts of the world that grow great garlic and make wonderful aioli."

After her first book, A Cook's Tour of Sonoma County *(Aris Books, Addison-Wesley 1990), Jordan published books about oil and vinegar, mustard, tomatoes, and pastas (Williams-Sonoma Collection, Weldon-Owen, Inc.) and polenta (Broadway Books). Harvard Common Press will be publishing her* California Home Cooking *in 1997 and Broadway Books will be publishing* Salt and Pepper *in 1998.*

Brie with Strawberries, Chocolate, and Garlic

Serves 6 to 8

2 pints fresh, sweet strawberries,
   cleaned and cut in half

4 tablespoons granulated sugar

2 tablespoons butter

1 head garlic, cloves separated, peeled,
   and slivered

4 ounces bittersweet chocolate

2 (8-ounce) rounds of ripe brie,
   at room temperature

1 sweet French baguette, thinly sliced

Place strawberries in a bowl, sprinkle over them 2 tablespoons of the sugar. Toss berries lightly and refrigerate.

Preheat the oven to 300°. In a small ovenproof pan or skillet, melt the butter, add the garlic, shake to distribute it evenly, and then sprinkle the remaining sugar over the top. Place in oven until garlic is completely tender, about 20 minutes. Remove from oven and set aside.

Set the brie on a large flat serving platter. In a double boiler, melt the chocolate. Carefully fold in the slivered garlic and pour the mixture over both rounds of brie. Spoon the strawberries and their juice onto the platter, not on top of the chocolate sauce but surrounding it. Arrange baguette slices on the edge of the platter or in a separate basket. Serve immediately.

I suggest for this recipe a mild but tasty garlic, such as Inchelium Red or Chet's Italian Red.

Inchelium Red

THE LARK CREEK INN
Bradley Ogden, Owner and Executive Chef

The James Beard Society voted Bradley Ogden "Best California Chef of 1993." He went on to *achieve other honors such as* Nation's Restaurant News *"Fine Dining Hall of Fame" award in 1994;* Where *magazine's "Silver Spoon Award" for best hospitality and service of 1995;* Zagat Survey's *commendation as "Best American Restaurant in Bay Area";* Restaurant Hospitality *magazine's "Best American Wine List";* Wine Spectator's *"Award of Excellence," and* San Francisco Focus *magazine's Reader's Choice Awards, "Best Newcomer of 1996," East Bay.*

The Lark Creek Inn began when Bradley and Jody Ogden and Michael and Leslye Dellar joined forces in 1988 to acquire and remodel the Lark Creek Inn in Larkspur, California.

The restaurant opened in August 1989 and was hailed almost immediately for its commitment to the highest standards of hospitality, service, and culinary excellence. Food and Wine *magazine wrote: "The best home cooking you can imagine, updated and lightened."* The New York Times *said, "Mr. Ogden's gutsy country cooking makes the drive from downtown San Francisco worthwhile."*

Grits and Garlic Custard

Serves 6

$1/4$ cup uncooked corn grits

$3/4$ cup milk

1 cup heavy cream

$1/2$ teaspoon minced garlic

$1/4$ teaspoon freshly ground black pepper

$3/4$ teaspoon kosher salt

2 eggs

Pinch of nutmeg

Preheat oven to 300°. In a small saucepan, combine grits, milk, $1/4$ cup cream, garlic, pepper, and $1/4$ teaspoon salt. Simmer slowly over low heat, covered, for 15 minutes. Remove from heat, uncover, and cool. In a small bowl, mix together the remaining $3/4$ cup cream, eggs, $1/2$ teaspoon salt, and nutmeg. Butter 6 3-ounce timbale molds. Place 2 tablespoons of cooked grits in each mold. Fill each mold to the top with egg custard mixture. Place molds in a baking pan and add enough hot water to the pan to come halfway up the molds. Bake for 20 minutes or until set. Let cool for 5 minutes before removing from timbale molds onto plates and serving.

I recommend for this dish a moderately hot garlic, such as Israeli or the Yugoslavian Red, which is spicy at first but mellows to a warm, sweet aftertaste.

YUGOSLAVIAN RED
Hardneck Rocambole

Seed from Dacha Barinka in British Columbia via Filaree Farm. Very large copper-veined, purple-blotched bulbs with 9 to 14 dark brown cloves. Hot and spicy flavor at first but not overwhelming, mellows to warm, pleasant, sweet aftertaste.

Stuffed Poblano Chiles with Roasted Garlic Sauce

Serves 4

2 heads garlic

4 tablespoons olive oil

2 tablespoons water

Kosher salt and freshly ground
    black pepper to taste

3/4 cup white wine

1/4 cup chicken stock

2 shallots, peeled and thinly sliced

1/2 cup cream

4 fresh poblano chiles

1/4 cup pine nuts

1/4 teaspoon chopped fresh thyme
    (or a pinch of dried)

2/3 cup fresh goat cheese

2 tablespoons chopped parsley

2 tablespoons chopped fresh basil

Preheat oven to 350°. Cut heads of garlic in half horizontally. Place in a small baking dish and drizzle with 1 tablespoon olive oil and 2 tablespoons water. Season lightly with salt and pepper. Cover tightly with foil and bake for about 30 minutes, or until tender. If the garlic starts to burn before it is soft, add a little water to the pan. Remove from the oven and let cool. When the garlic is cool enough to handle, squeeze the soft pulp from the heads into a small saucepan. Add the white wine, chicken stock, and shallots and bring to a simmer over medium heat. Cover the pan, reduce heat, and simmer for 10 to 15 minutes. Add the cream, bring to a slow boil over medium heat, and stir to reduce the sauce until it coats the back of a spoon, about 3 minutes. Season with salt and pepper and set aside. The sauce can be made hours in advance and refrigerated when cool.

Roast and peel the chiles. Leaving the stem on, cut a small slit in the side of each chile and remove the seeds. Heat 1 tablespoon olive oil in a small sauté pan over low heat. Add the pine nuts and toast to a golden brown, tossing frequently so they will not burn, about 3 minutes. When the pine nuts are done, add the thyme, toss to mix, and remove from the pan. Set aside to cool. Place the goat cheese in a small bowl and stir until smooth. Mix in the pine nuts, herbs, and salt and pepper to taste. Stuff the chiles carefully with the cheese mixture. Fold over the opening and place seam side down on a lightly oiled baking pan. Drizzle with the remaining 2 tablespoons of olive oil. Refrigerate until 15 minutes before serving.

Preheat the oven to 350°. Place the pan of peppers in the oven and bake for about 15 minutes or until just warmed through. Reheat the garlic sauce and spoon onto warm serving plates. Place a stuffed pepper in the center of each plate.

For this recipe, I recommend a hot earthy garlic like the Georgian La Panant Kari or the German Floha, which is especially fine for roasting.

LA PANANT KARI
Hardneck Artichoke

Seed from David Caravagnaro at Seed Savers. From the Republic of Georgia. Small to moderate bulbs, 8 to 12 cloves. Hot, hot, hot. After heat dissipates, it has the usual Georgian taste: rich, heavy, earthy.

GIOVANNI LEONI

Giovanni is a dear personal friend with a golden heart. He and his wife, Michelle, live on a small farm in northern California. Until 1994 when he retired, he was owner and chef at Vanessi's and Buca Giovanni, famed landmarks in North Beach, San Francisco. Born in the Serchio Valley in Tuscany, Leoni was honored with a gold medal for his contributions to the growing fame of Italian cuisine. After he came to San Francisco, he was acclaimed by chefs and reviewers and colleagues as "…a true Artisan of the Culinary Art…the Maestro approaches his profession with a mixture of scholarship, skill, hard work, and sure pleasure that separates great chefs from competent cooks…. He has educated San Franciscans in the subtle delights and goodness of Tuscan cooking years before they traveled to Italy and discovered its roots…." At Buca Giovanni, Leoni "…not only served homemade pasta, homegrown rabbit and vegetables from his own ranch, he even roasted his own coffee."

GERMAN RED
Hardneck Rocambole

Seed via Filaree Farm from old-time Idaho gardeners of German descent. Very vigorous. Large bulbs with large light-brown cloves tinged with faint purple at base. Strong, hot, spicy flavor.

Sweet and Sour Garlic

Serves 2 to 3

1 1/4 tablespoon extra virgin olive oil

3 heads garlic cloves, peeled

1 1/2 jalapeño pepper (optional)

3/4 tablespoon honey

1 1/2 tablespoons balsamic vinegar

1 1/2 tablespoons water

Salt and freshly ground black pepper to taste

In a nonstick sauté pan over medium low heat, add oil, garlic, and jalapeño if desired. Sauté until golden brown, about 3 minutes. Add honey and sauté slowly for 2 more minutes. (Take care not to burn.) Add vinegar, and sauté 30 seconds. Add water, sauté 1 1/2 minutes more. Add salt and pepper. Mix and serve.

For this sweet garlic dish, use tasty German Red.

Linguine with Garlic and Sage

Serves 2 to 4

3 quarts salted water

8 ounces linguine, preferably imported from Italy

2 tablespoons extra virgin olive oil

12 fresh sage leaves, finely chopped

6 or more cloves garlic, finely chopped

1 to 2 jalapeño peppers, chopped (optional)

2 tablespoons grated Parmesan cheese

Salt and freshly ground black pepper

Bring water to a boil in a large stockpot. Add linguine and cook for 10 to 12 minutes, or until al dente. Meanwhile, add olive oil to heavy-bottomed sauté pan and place over medium heat. Add sage, garlic, and chiles, if desired. Sauté until garlic starts to brown, about 20 seconds. Immediately add 4 tablespoons water taken from the boiling pasta. Add cheese and salt and pepper to taste. Drain the pasta. Toss pasta and sauce and serve.

Use a sweet, mild garlic, like Inchelium Red.

LE MANOIR AUX QUAT'SAISONS
Raymond Blanc, Executive Chef/Owner

Raymond Blanc arrived in Great Britain in the early seventies. He opened his first restaurant, Les Quat'Saisons, in 1977 in Summertown. The restaurant was awarded its first Michelin star in 1978 and its second in 1983.

Blanc Restaurants, established in 1984, included Le Manoir aux Quat'Saisons. Le Manoir has received the highest awards in virtually all of the guides and is the only establishment in Great Britain to hold both the Gold and Red Relais & Chateaux shields.

In addition to these accomplishments, Blanc has contributed to many books, newspapers, and magazines. He has written four cookbooks, one of which was accompanied by a BBC2 TV series. His most recent publication is A Blanc Christmas. *The following recipes are reprinted with permission from* Blanc Mange, *published by BBC Books.*

ARMENIAN
Hardneck Rocambole

Seed from Silva Baghdassarian, in the Armenian village of Hadrut Karabagh. One of the largest-bulbed and most intense garlics in my collection. Bulbs firm and white with rose to purple stripes. Extremely tough and durable leaves and stalks. Strong, earthy flavor. Ideal for roasting. One of my favorites.

Bread Rolls Filled with Wild Mushrooms

Serves 4

4 round, good-quality white bread rolls

2 large garlic cloves, peeled and halved

$1/4$ cup olive oil

7 ounces wild mushrooms

2 tablespoons unsalted butter

$1/4$ cup water mixed with $1\,1/2$ teaspoons
   freshly squeezed lemon juice

Salt and freshly ground black pepper
   to taste

1 teaspoon chopped fresh chervil

A few tarragon leaves, blanched in boiling
   water for 10 seconds, then chopped

1 teaspoon chopped fresh parsley

$1/4$ cup whipping cream, whipped

Preheat oven to 350°. To prepare the bread rolls, slice off the top of each roll about one-third of the way down. Scoop out soft insides. Rub inside of hollow and top inside of "lid" with garlic. Brush olive oil over the same surfaces. Place rolls in the oven on the rack to dry out and crisp for 10 minutes.

To prepare the mushroom filling, in a small sauté pan, sauté the wild mushrooms in the butter for 1 minute. Add the water and lemon juice mixture and cook for 1 more minute, covered. Season to taste with salt and pepper, and hold in reserve.

Add chopped herbs to whipped cream. Season with salt and pepper to taste. Just before serving, whisk whipped cream into the mushrooms with their juices. Divide mushrooms among the 4 rolls. Spoon sauce on and around each roll. Top with the "lids" and serve.

With wild mushrooms or other delicately flavored earth-foods, I recommend a rich but not hot garlic like Armenian or Xian.

Roasted Pork Fillets with Onion and Garlic Purée

Serves 4

4 tablespoons unsalted butter

2 (14-ounce) pork (or veal) fillets, trimmed of all fat

11 ounces pork spare ribs, chopped into very small pieces

1 clove garlic, peeled and chopped

1 sprig fresh thyme

Salt and freshly ground black pepper to taste

7/8 cup water

Onion and Garlic Purée (recipe follows)

Preheat oven to 350°. On medium heat on the stovetop, in a small roasting tray, heat butter until it foams. Sear and brown the fillets and the spareribs on all sides for approximately 10 minutes until both fillets and bones are a beautifully golden brown. (The spareribs must be cut into very small pieces so they lend their flavor more readily and the simmering time will be shortened.) Add garlic and thyme, season with salt and pepper. Roast in the oven for 5 to 7 minutes. Remove fillets to a serving platter, season again with salt and pepper, and keep warm by covering with aluminum foil.

To make the sauce, place the roasting tray over medium heat on the stovetop. Add water and bring to a boil. Scrape bottom of pan to deglaze and dilute all caramelized juices. Simmer for 5 minutes before straining into a large, flameproof casserole. On high heat, reduce liquid for 5 minutes, until you have a little over half a cup. Taste and correct seasoning. (Reseasoning is necessary because the brief cooking times mean that the seasoning will not have had time to permeate the meat.) Hold in reserve.

To serve, prepare or reheat Onion and Garlic Purée. Pour the liquid, released from the foil-wrapped fillets, into the sauce being held in reserve. Heat through. Reheat fillets in the 350° oven for 2 minutes if necessary. Carve fillets into thin slices and arrange on a warm serving dish. Pour sauce over fillet slices and serve with onion and garlic purée separately. Or spread purée on the middle of each plate, fan meat slices over, and serve sauce separately.

I recommend with pork or veal a strong and moderately hot garlic such as Russian Sanctuary or French Messadrone.

FRENCH MESSADRONE
Softneck Silverskin

Original stock from David Cavagnaro at Seed Savers. Moderate-to-large bulb with average-sized white-to-tan skinned cloves. Sharp when raw, but simple, smooth, and nutty when cooked.

ONION AND GARLIC PURÉE

Serves 4

12 large cloves garlic, peeled

3 1/2 cups water

2 large onions, peeled and chopped

1/4 cup olive oil

4 sprigs fresh thyme

7 tablespoons double cream

1/4 cup extra virgin olive oil

Salt and freshly ground white pepper
to taste

Cut garlic cloves in half lengthwise. Remove and discard central green germ, which is bitter. Simmer garlic in water for 12 to 15 minutes. Drain well and reserve. In a covered cast-iron pan on low heat, sweat the onion in olive oil for 15 to 20 minutes. Do not brown. Stir occasionally. Add garlic, thyme, and cream. Cook for 10 more minutes. Cool and remove the thyme. Liquefy to a purée. Enrich with extra virgin olive oil. Adjust seasonings to taste. (This purée can be prepared a day in advance.)

With its brother allium, I recommend a hot, tangy garlic like Purple Cauldron.

OLIVETO
Paul Bertolli, Chef/Owner

Before becoming chef and owner of Oliveto, in Oakland, California, Paul Bertolli traveled widely and worked in Italy. For ten years, he served as Executive Chef at Chez Panisse in Berkeley, California.

Committed to collecting or making, as much as possible, his own ingredients, he now makes the vinegars for the restaurant, including an aged aceto balsamico. *He often comes to the kitchen laden with wild fennel, bay, sage, or mustard, with crabs he himself caught in San Francisco Bay, or with local vine prunings to fuel the grill. The kitchen makes its own prosciutto and salami from meats Bertolli selects.*

Bertolli has written the successful book Chez Panisse Cooking *and has received a variety of honors, including 1985* Esquire's *register of "Men and Women Under 40 Who Are Changing the Nation" and* San Francisco Focus *magazine's 1989 "Chef of the Year." He has been cited by several critics as one of the two or three top chefs in the country.*

Oliveto's basic menu changes with the seasons, four times yearly. Once a month, the restaurant offers special dinners created to complement special ingredients, such as local garlics, Tuscan or Piedmontese wines, Italian truffles, or heirloom tomatoes.

Note: Young garlic plants can be found in gourmet markets in early springtime (or, of course, grown in your garden.)

Spring Garlic Soup

Serves 10

3 tablespoons olive oil

10 ounces young garlic plants (10 to 15 plants), white part only, cut coarsely

1 cup water

1 pound 6 ounces Red Rose potatoes, peeled and quartered

1 1/2 quarts fresh chicken broth

1/2 cup heavy cream

1 1/2 teaspoons sea salt

2 1/2 teaspoons champagne vinegar

1 loaf sourdough bread

1 tablespoon garlic-infused olive oil

Freshly ground black pepper to taste

Warm the olive oil in a 6-quart noncorroding pot. Add the garlic plants and half the water. Bring to a simmer, cover tightly, and cook for 15 minutes. Add potatoes and remaining water. Cook at a simmer for another 15 minutes. Add chicken broth, cover the pot, and allow to bubble gently 20 minutes or more. Purée the soup in a blender. Pass the purée through a medium-fine sieve into a large bowl. Stir in cream and salt. Add vinegar.

To make sourdough croutons, preheat oven to 350°. Cut bread into small cubes, toss them in oil, and bake until very crisp, about 15 minutes, shaking pan several times to ensure even browning.

Reheat the soup gently and serve it in warm bowls. Grind black pepper over each portion and serve with croutons.

For this soup, I recommend garlic plants that are hot and rich even in the early cloves and greens, such as either California Late or Mazatlàn.

New Potatoes and Spring Garlic Ravioli al Frantoio

Serves 8 to 10

There is perhaps no better foil for the flavor of newly pressed olive oil than potatoes, used here as a basis for a stuffing for ravioli. The potatoes are perfumed with garlic picked in the early season before it forms a head. Most spring garlic has none of the pungency of mature, cured garlic.

POTATO-GARLIC FILLING

10 to 12 tablespoons fruity extra virgin olive oil

1 pound spring garlic plants, white and pale green parts only, cleaned and diced

1/2 cup water

2 pounds new potatoes, such as Red Rose

1 teaspoon salt

Freshly ground black pepper to taste

1 teaspoon white wine or champagne vinegar

2 tablespoons minced fresh chives

1/2 cup freshly grated Parmigiano Reggiano

Warm 2 tablespoons of the olive oil in a 3-quart heavy-bottomed stockpot. Add the garlic and 1/2 cup water. Cover pot and sweat the garlic until tender, about 10 minutes. Add potatoes and cover with 1 quart water. Bring to a boil, reduce to simmer, and cook until potatoes are tender, about 12 minutes. Drain potatoes in a colander, then rice them through the fine blade of a food mill. Add the salt, a little freshly ground pepper, the vinegar, chives, and Parmigiano.

2 cups all-purpose flour

2 large fresh eggs

Place flour in bowl and make a well in the center. Add eggs and, using a fork, stir yolks and whites together to blend. If dough does not adhere to itself, add a little water. Continue mixing until dough forms a rough ball. Turn out onto a lightly floured work surface and knead for 8 minutes. Wrap dough in a towel and let rest for 30 minutes.

Divide dough in half. Using a pasta machine, roll $1/2$ of the dough to thin, almost transparent ribbons roughly $5 1/2$ inches wide, 15 inches long. Store sheets floured (so they don't stick) and slightly overlapping, under a towel. Set a sheet of dough in front of you. Have ready a small bowl of water. Along the length, place scant tablespoons of filling in neat balls 1 inch from the bottom and side edges and 1 inch apart. Moisten bottom edges of sheet and the spaces between balls. (An atomizer is quicker: Direct a fine mist over the entire surface.) With both hands, fold the sheet so the top and bottom edges meet evenly. Flatten and seal spaces between each ravioli with thumb and forefingers, as close as possible to the stuffing, expelling any pockets of air at the unsealed end. Press top and bottom edges together so they seal. Use a zigzag ravioli wheel to cut out the ravioli. Cut directly through the sealed sheets, about $3/8$-inch from the filling, creating squares $2 1/2$ inches wide. Check all sides for a good seal. If any edges are unsealed, moisten your fingers and press together. Set the ravioli in one layer on floured plates. Refrigerate until ready to use.

Warm 8 to 10 large pasta bowls. Bring a large pot (about 2 gallons) of water to boil. For every gallon of water, add $1 1/2$ tablespoons salt. Toss in the ravioli. Cook for about 5 minutes, then drain in a colander. Using a large slotted spoon, carefully transfer ravioli to the bowls. Drizzle 1 tablespoon extra virgin olive oil over and around the ravioli. Serve at once.

For these ravioli, I recommend a rich Armenian garlic.

RESTAURANT DELMONICO
Angie Brown and Rose Marie Dietrich, Owners

Restaurant Delmonico opened its doors on the corner of St. Charles Avenue and Erato Street in New Orleans in 1895, borrowing its name from New York's Delmonico's. Purchased by Anthony La Franca in 1911, Restaurant Delmonico has been operated by his family since that time. Much of its current menu was created by Anthony's widow, Marie Masset La Franca. Daughters Angie Brown and Rose Marie Dietrich carry on the tradition of warm, southern hospitality. With an easygoing pace reflective of the fine New Orleans dining of the early years, the restaurant offers one of the most varied menus in New Orleans, with a selection of seafood, fowl, and meat. Still containing the appearance and charm of an old New Orleans home, the main dining rooms have retained their seventeen-foot ceilings, mahogany wainscoting, and chandeliers with, behind the bar, a large mural by John McCrady depicting life on the Mississippi River in the 1860s. A variety of other private areas—the Rose Room, the Anthony Room, the Crystal Room, the Sitting Room, the Cornstalk Room—offer spaces for small or large gatherings.

Delmonico Baked Creole Eggplant

Serves 4 to 6

2 eggplants, peeled and diced

1 onion, chopped

2 stalks celery, chopped

1 cup small shrimp (4 to 6 ounces), cooked

2 tablespoons butter or oil

1 tomato, chopped

Dash of Tabasco sauce

Dash of Worcestershire sauce

1 bay leaf

$^1/_4$ cup seasoned bread crumbs

1 clove garlic, chopped

Preheat oven to 350°. In a medium saucepan, parboil eggplant. In a skillet over medium heat, sauté onion, celery, and shrimp in butter for 2 minutes. Add chopped tomato and cook for another minute. Add Tabasco, Worcestershire, and bay leaf. When all ingredients are melted and blended together, fold in eggplant.

Place in baking dish. Top with seasoned bread crumbs. Bake in oven for approximately 20 minutes. Remove bay leaf before serving.

I recommend for this dish a hearty, hot, heavy garlic such as California Late or Celaya Purple.

CELAYA PURPLE
Hardneck Rocambole

From Mexico; seed from Filaree Farm. Large bulbs often oddly shaped, with skins of large cloves occasionally dark purple. Raw taste fiery with nice finish.

Crawfish Étouffée

Serves 4

$1/2$ cup vegetable oil

2 large onions, chopped

2 stalks celery, chopped

$1/3$ cup chopped bell pepper

2 cloves garlic, chopped

2 tomatoes, chopped

Salt and freshly ground black pepper to taste

3 cups crawfish tails in the shell
(about 1 pound)

4 cups steamed rice

Heat oil in a heavy skillet. Add onions, celery, bell pepper, and garlic. Brown on medium heat until onions are transparent, about 5 minutes. Add tomatoes and cook for 5 minutes. Add salt and pepper to taste. Add crawfish and cook for 5 minutes. Serve over steamed rice.

I recommend a garlic mild enough not to override the taste of the crawfish, but hot enough to add tang, such as German Red or Persian Star.

PERSIAN STAR
Hardneck Purple Stripe

Seed from John Swenson via Filaree Farm. Purchased at a bazaar in Samarkand, Uzbekistan. Outer bulb wrapper sometimes smooth white but inner wrappers purple-streaked. Cloves red-tipped with background of marbled streaks. Pleasant flavor, with a mild spicy zing.

RESTAURANT LULU
Jody Denton, Executive Chef

Denton's nearly twenty years as a professional cook (including two years' training in Switzerland) have taken him around the United States and to Europe. A native of Austin, Texas, Denton has worked in top restaurants, including Wolfgang Puck's Eureka Restaurant and Brewery (Los Angeles), Mark Miller's Red Sage (Washington, D.C.) and the Eccentric (Chicago), The Big Bowl Cafe (Chicago), and the Mansion on Turtle Creek (Dallas).

Denton's specialties, in addition to his Provençal creations for LuLu, include the food from Asian, Latin, and Caribbean cultures. Not at all fond of fusion cuisine, Denton prefers the pure flavors that come from each region, wherever he might be. This is an explanation for his use, at Restaurant LuLu, of "…as much as possible the seasonally fresh ingredients from right here in California."

The menu at San Francisco's Restaurant LuLu often changes five times a week, reflecting the current crop of produce, the latest catch of fish, or the availability of top-quality fresh meat and game.

(recipe follows…)

Roasted Garlic and Goat Cheese Ravioli with Baby Spinach, Currants, and Pine Nuts

Serves 4 to 6

3 heads garlic

1 cup mild goat cheese

$1/4$ cup aged goat cheese, such as *crotin*
   or *bucheron*

$1/2$ cup extra virgin olive oil

2 teaspoons chopped fresh mint

1 teaspoon chopped fresh marjoram

1 teaspoon salt

$1/2$ teaspoon freshly ground black pepper

1 pound very thin fresh pasta sheets

1 egg yolk

$1/4$ cup butter

2 cups baby spinach

$1/4$ cup currants

$1/4$ cup toasted pine nuts

Preheat oven to 350°. Peel most of the outer skin from garlic heads. Cut off first inch of the top, exposing clove tips. Wrap garlic heads in foil and place in the oven for about 45 minutes. Allow heads to cool and remove from foil. Press the heads to squeeze out the soft roasted garlic. Set aside. In a mixing bowl, combine roasted garlic, goat cheeses, olive oil, mint, marjoram, salt, and pepper. Mix with a wooden spoon until smooth and well combined.

On a lightly floured table, lay out sheeted pasta in strips $1^1/_2$ to 2 inches wide. Mix egg yolk with a little water and lightly brush surface of one strip. Spoon dollops of the cheese mixture at about $1^1/_2$- to 2-inch intervals. Lay another strip gently on top of first. Gently seal edges and then seal between the dollops of cheese until all the pasta around the cheese is sealed. Cut between the cheese to form the individual ravioli. Dust with flour, cover with a towel, and let sit until ready to serve. If making the ravioli in advance, cover them well in a single layer on a cookie sheet and refrigerate until ready for use. Bring 2 quarts salted water to a boil in a stockpot. Drop in ravioli and cook for about 4 to 6 minutes depending on the thickness of the pasta. When they are nearly done, place a sauté pan with the butter, spinach, currants, and pine nuts over medium heat. Before the butter melts completely, with a slotted spoon, put the cooked ravioli in the pan and add about $^1/_4$ cup of the pasta-cooking water. Gently toss ravioli around in the pan until the butter has completely melted and the ravioli are glazed. Serve immediately.

With the strength and variation of tastes in cheeses and herbs here, I recommend a large, earthy garlic. One of the best for roasting is Siberian.

Siberian

RESTAURANT SWIETOSZEK
Andrzej Smagna, Chef, Director

Swietoszek is located in a vaulted basement, one of the few to survive the Warsaw Uprising of World War II. The restaurant is the headquarters of the Union of Professional Art and Culture. Frequented by actors and artists, the candlelit interior is a Warsaw favorite.

Spanish Roja

Grilled Trout

Serves 5

5 fresh trout (about $1/2$ pound each)

Juice of 2 freshly squeezed lemons

$2 1/2$ teaspoons salt

Freshly ground black pepper to taste

5 eggs, hard-boiled

$3/4$ cup butter

12 cloves garlic, peeled and crushed

$1/4$ cup chopped fresh parsley

$1/4$ cup chopped fresh dill

1 teaspoon fresh thyme leaves

Clean trout and pat dry. Sprinkle both sides of each trout with lemon juice. Sprinkle $1/2$ teaspoon salt on both sides of each trout. Use pepper to taste on each trout. Reserve trout while preparing the stuffing.

Grate the 5 eggs into a bowl. Add crushed garlic cloves to eggs. Add butter and parsley. Add salt and pepper to taste. Mix thoroughly.

Stuff each trout. Sprinkle with thyme. Wrap in foil. Roast on the grill, 8 minutes on each side.

I recommend for this and most (but not all) fish dishes a moderately rich garlic that is not hot, such as California Early, or Persian Star, which is hot at first and zingy.

Veal with Garlic and Herbs

Serves 4 to 6

$1/2$ teaspoon salt

10 cloves garlic, peeled and crushed

2 pounds veal roast

1 teaspoon fresh thyme

1 teaspoon fresh marjoram

Preheat oven to 400°. Add salt to crushed garlic cloves. Rub mixture over the entire roast. Sprinkle roast with combined herbs. Roast, uncovered, in the oven for $1 1/2$ hours. Serve cold or hot.

For this dish, I recommend a strong garlic that is moderately hot and with a lingering taste that fades fast, such as Creole Red or Spanish Roja.

ROSE PISTOLA
Scott Warner, Executive Chef

As a young man, Warner spent his summer vacations in Europe, where his mother attended Parisian cooking classes. By the time he entered the University of Southern California as a music major, Warner was catering to earn his living.

He spent several years cooking in small New York bistros, then returned to Röckenwagner in Los Angeles, where he was Day Chef for three years.

In 1994 he made his way up the coast to San Francisco and Restaurant Lulu, where he soon became Sous Chef under Chef Reed Hearon.

Reed Hearon, San Francisco Focus *magazine's 1996 Chef of the Year, had worked at several southwestern restaurants, including Mark Miller's Coyote Cafe in Santa Fe, New Mexico. His first culinary love is the authentic Mexican cuisine of the Oaxaca, Yucatan, and Vera Cruz regions. He has published one book, and is about to publish a second.*

Warner and Hearon traveled together through Liguria, the Italian region that inspires Rose Pistola's food and personifies the vibrancy of the restaurant's eighty-eighty-year-old namesake. In 1996 Hearon appointed Warner Executive Chef at Rose Pistola.

Note: Young galric plants often show up in gourmet groceries and farmers' markets in early spring.

Garlic-Crusted Roast Crab

Serves 4

1 quart (1 to 1 1/2 pounds) white garlic
  cloves (or young garlic plants
  if available)

2 bunches parsley

1 bunch fresh thyme

1/2 cup coarsely ground toasted
  fennel seed

1/2 cup crushed red pepper flakes

1 quart olive oil

1/4 cup salt

4 Dungeness crabs, parboiled for 8 minutes
  in salted water, cleaned and cracked
  (save shell for plate garnish)

Clarified butter

Preheat oven (preferably wood-fired) to 400°.
Chop garlic and herbs finely, then mix with spices and
oil. Cover crabs generously with this marinade and roast
in hot oven until golden brown, about 10 minutes. Hold
crabs to rest in a warm place for 5 minutes.

Reheat crabs in oven for a few minutes, then cut
into sections between legs. Reassemble on plate with
the shell.

Serve with clarified butter.

I recommend for this dish, so the fine taste of crab and
ocean is not lost, a mild almost sweet garlic, such as
Inchelium Red or Chet's Italian Red, both from Washington State.

Chet's Italian Red

Ravioli of Green Garlic and Ricotta with Sautéed Tender Greens

Serves 4 to 6

PASTA

- 2 1/2 pounds (8 3/4 cups) all-purpose flour
- 2 teaspoons salt
- 2 eggs
- 1/2 bottle dry white wine
- 2 tablespoons olive oil

In a large bowl, mix together flour and salt. In a separate bowl, whisk together eggs, wine, and olive oil. Make a well in center of the flour, add wet ingredients. Stir with a fork until it holds together. Turn dough out onto a lightly floured work surface and knead until smooth. Cover and let dough rest in refrigerator for at least 1 hour. The dough can also be made in a mixer with a dough hook attachment.

Acropolis

RAVIOLI FILLING

1 egg

1 quart ricotta cheese

1 cup finely chopped garlic greens

1 tablespoon grated lemon zest

Salt and freshly ground black pepper to taste

1 bunch young dandelion greens
    or arugula

Olive oil

$1/4$ cup freshly grated Parmesan cheese

Whisk egg and combine with ricotta cheese, garlic, lemon zest, and salt and pepper to taste. Cut strips of dough to fit your pasta maker; roll out sheets quite thin. Fill raviolis according to instructions for your machine. Dust ravioli with flour to prevent them from sticking together and hold in refrigerator until serving. If more ravioli are made than are needed to serve immediately they can be stored in freezer.

To serve, drop ravioli in boiling, salted water. Meanwhile over medium heat wilt the greens in a sauté pan with olive oil and salt and pepper to taste. When ravioli float to surface of boiling water, remove them with a pasta strainer. Toss ravioli in the pan with the greens and a few drops of the pasta water. Add just enough water to emulsify with the olive oil. Serve with a light sprinkle of Parmesan cheese on top.

Taste varies less among greens of different garlic varieties than do the cured bulbs. But still not wanting to ride over the stringent taste of the garden greens, I recommend the spring stalks of a strong garlic: Mexican, Metechi, or Acropolis.

THE STINKING ROSE
Jerry Dal Bozzo and son Dean, Vince Bigone, Jr., Dante Serafini, Partners
Jeffrey Acuna, Chef

In 1991 Jerry Dal Bozzo, together with his long-time friends, created The Stinking Rose, a Garlic Restaurant, which opened its doors in San Francisco on July 3, 1991. A second location has since opened on La Cienega Boulevard in Beverly Hills.

Jerry Dal Bozzo is Ex Officio President of the North Beach Chamber of Commerce, the merchants' association for San Francisco's "Little Italy of the West."

Dean, Jerry's son and partner, served as Cook at Fog City Diner.

Another partner, Vince Bigone, Jr., grew up on Potrero Hill in San Francisco. At Santa Clara University he was an All-American baseball player. The following four years, he played for the California Angels.

Dante Serafini was born and raised in North Beach. His family has been in the restaurant business many years. His father owned the original North Beach Caffe.

The menu at The Stinking Rose features recipes reflecting Northern Italy's nuova cucina, *with a strong influence from contemporary California cuisine.*

When Great Britain's Queen Elizabeth II recently pronounced garlic unpleasant to the royal palate, The Stinking Rose issued a press release banning Her Majesty from the premises.

San Francisco's Stinking Rose Restaurant, which consumes 3 1/2 tons of garlic every month, as well as 12,000 mints, received a tribute in a major garlic article in Smithsonian *magazine's December 1995 issue.*

Forty-Clove Garlic Chicken with Carbernet Sauce and Wild Mushroom-Roast Garlic Bread Pudding

Serves 4

1 frying chicken (about 4 or 5 pounds), cut in pieces

$^1/_3$ cup olive oil

Coarse salt and freshly ground black pepper to taste

40 cloves garlic, peeled

1 sprig fresh rosemary, finely chopped

In a large bowl, toss chicken pieces with olive oil, garlic, rosemary, and salt and pepper to taste. Cover and refrigerate for 1 to 2 hours. Preheat oven to 400°. Place chicken and garlic in a baking dish and bake, covered, for 30 minutes. Uncover and bake 10 minutes more.

For this dish, I recommend a strong, rich garlic that is not too hot—Kitab.

CABERNET SAUCE

5 tablespoons butter

1 onion, diced

2 $^1/_2$ cups cabernet sauvignon

2 $^1/_2$ cups chicken stock or beef broth

$^1/_2$ cup cream

1 teaspoon coarse salt

Freshly ground black pepper to taste

While chicken roasts, heat 2 tablespoons butter in a large saucepan. Add onion. Cook, stirring, for 2 minutes. Add wine and reduce liquid by two-thirds. Add chicken stock and cream. Cook, stirring, to reduce by half, about 5 minutes. Add salt and pepper to taste. Whisk in 3 tablespoons butter. Strain sauce and reserve.

Wild Mushroom–Roast Garlic Bread Pudding

Serves 4

2 tablespoons butter

$1/2$ pound wild mushrooms, sliced

1 tablespoon minced celery

1 tablespoon minced onion

1 teaspoon chopped fresh herbs
(oregano, tarragon, thyme)

$1\,^3/_4$ cups heavy cream

3 eggs plus 1 egg yolk

1 tablespoon roasted garlic purée
(see Tips, page 52)

1 cup cubed bread (French, focaccia,
or brioche)

Salt and freshly ground black pepper
to taste

Heat butter in large saucepan. Add mushrooms, celery, and onions. Sauté 3 minutes. Add fresh herbs. Stir in cream. Slowly whip in eggs, the extra yolk, and roasted garlic purée. Add cubed bread and toss well. Let mixture sit for 30 minutes.

Preheat oven to 350°. Pour bread mixture into 4 buttered ramekins and cover with foil. Place ramekins in baking dish and fill with water halfway up sides of ramekins. Bake until custard is set and a toothpick comes out clean, about 25 minutes.

To serve, unmold pudding at the top of plate. In middle of the plate, place chicken, with cabernet sauce drizzled over it.

For the purée, I suggest the garlic perfect for roasting: the Siberian, with its large, solid, rich cloves or the German Floha.

ADDITIONAL VARIETIES

ISRAELI
Hardneck Rocambole

Seed from Michigan collector Ed Spaans via Filaree Farm. When grown well in temperate climates, the bulbs are large, with dark, thin, red veins and purple blotches. Its 4 to 9 cloves range from light brown to mahogany. Sharp but rich flavor, occasionally even sweet.

JAPANESE
Softneck Artichoke

Bulbs, often finely striped, can grow almost as large as those of the so-called elephant garlic, with 5 to 7 large, yellow-tan cloves. From Filaree Farm via an elderly Japanese farmer in western Washington. Sharp but not extremely hot, with lingering rich taste.

KITAB
Hardneck Purple Stripe (marbled group)

From a mountainside above Kitab, Uzbekistan, via Filaree Farm. Very large bulbs with large fat cloves spotted with brown and purple. Often mistaken for Rocambole but has fewer cloves to a bulb (4 to 6) and stores longer. Exceptionally strong and rich flavor without excessive heat.

KOREAN ROCAMBOLE
Hardneck Continental

From South Korea, via New Mexico and Southern Exposure Seed Exchange in Virginia. A typical Rocambole, its scape often makes 2 complete curls. Bulb is moderate in size with 8 to 10 cloves. Can be hot hot hot!

LENINGRAD
Hardneck Porcelain

Similar to Romanian Red. Plants are tall and dark green; large symmetrical bulbs have 4 to 6 very plump cloves and are easy to clean. A clean, hot taste that lingers.

MCHADIDZHVARI
Softneck Rocambole

From the Republic of Georgia. Medium-to-large bulbs, often oddly shaped, with 6 to 10 moderately sized cloves. Like many Georgian garlics, it has a rich, meaty taste that can be sharp.

EL TOPIL
Señora Soledad Diaz Altamirano

Louis Segal and his wife, Susan, visited friends in Oaxaca, Mexico. They ran across what they described in our phone conversation as a fine restaurant owned by Señora Diaz Altamirano.

"We had a magnificent garlic soup," Louis said in that phone conversation. "We've gone back several times."

"Get the recipe," I said.

Louis proposed to Señora Diaz Altamirano that in exchange for her recipe, her soup could be included in a book his stepfather was writing about garlic. His stepfather would make the soup and, if it were as good as promised, he would include the recipe in his new book. She wrote out her recipe on scraps of paper. I've made the soup twice and it is indeed worth including.

ASIAN TEMPEST
Hardneck Purple Stripe (Marbled Group)

Seed from David Cavaragnaro at Seed Savers Exchange. Specific source unknown but definitely from Asia. Bulbs moderate to large, averaging 6 well-shaped cloves. Raw garlic is fiery but heat mellows to a pleasing finish.

Sopa de Ajo

Serves 5

1 pound red tomatoes, chopped

1 jalapeño or other hot green pepper, finely chopped

Pinch of cumin

4 cloves

10 cloves garlic, chopped, plus 10 whole cloves garlic

1 tablespoon olive oil

1 medium white onion, chopped

3 cups chicken broth

$1/4$ cup chopped mint, parsley, and celery (optional)

In a 2-quart stockpot, place the red tomatoes, the jalapeño, cumin, the 4 cloves, and 4 chopped garlic cloves over medium-high heat. Boil for 10 minutes. Set aside. In a skillet, heat the olive oil and sauté onion and 6 chopped garlic cloves; pour into tomato mix. Add 3 cups chicken broth and mix well. In a small pot, bring 1 quart water to boil. Put 10 garlic cloves into the water and boil for 4 minutes. Stir into chicken broth mixture. Chopped mint, parsley, and celery may be added and cooked 5 minutes more. Serve with slices of baguettes lightly fried with a favorite cheese.

I recommend for this recipe the very spicy hot Mexican or Asian Tempest garlic.

TANIA'S
Martha de J. and Elias Sanchez,
Owners and chefs

When she was nine years old, Martha de J. Sanchez came to the U.S., a refugee from Castro's Cuba. In 1969 her husband, Elias, escaped Cuba via Guantanamo Bay, the U.S. naval base.

Martha and Elias Sanchez describe themselves as two of over two million Cubans who migrated to the United States in the mass exodus known to Cubans as "the Freedom Flight."

Homesick for the food of their native Cuba, the Sanchez family opened a small cafe in the rear of their Chicago grocery store. Within a few months the restaurant had a faithful clientele, much of it non-Hispanic.

Today the small cafe is "...a sprawling, 416-seat restaurant named in honor of our daughter, Tania."

Martha and Elias Sanchez compare themselves to earlier immigrants "...who came to this country seeking refuge from oppression and hope for a better life. As was true for so many others, our dreams became reality."

Breast of Chicken
Siboney Style

Serves 4

This chicken makes an excellent entrée served with rice and black bean soup.

> **2 whole boneless, skinless chicken breasts, approximately 2 pounds total**
>
> **1 cup red wine**
>
> **4 tablespoons Spanish sherry vinegar (or balsamic vinegar)**
>
> **3 tablespoons olive oil**
>
> **6 cloves garlic, thinly sliced**
>
> **1 large onion, sliced**
>
> **Salt and freshly ground black pepper to taste**
>
> **2 slices low-sodium bacon, cut into strips**
>
> **1 1/2 cups sliced mushrooms**
>
> **2 tablespoons chopped fresh cilantro**
>
> **2 tablespoons fresh chopped flat-leaf parsley**
>
> **1 cup chicken stock**

Cut chicken breasts in half along the breastbone line. Place in a deep dish. Add the wine, the vinegar, and half the olive oil. Scatter the sliced garlic and half the onion slices over the meat. Season with salt and pepper to taste. Cover plate and refrigerate for 8 to 12 hours (or overnight), turning the chicken occasionally.

Preheat oven to 325°. Lift chicken breasts from the dish and pat dry, reserving the marinade. Heat remaining olive oil in a sauté pan and brown chicken breasts on all sides. Transfer to a baking pan. Add bacon and remaining onion to the sauté pan. Cook until the onion is soft, about 5 minutes. Stir in mushrooms and cook for about 3 minutes. Add reserved marinade and cook for 2 more minutes. Add the stock, cilantro, and parsley. Cover the chicken breasts with this sauce and bake for about 30 minutes. Transfer chicken breasts to serving dish. Boil remaining juices for a few minutes, to reduce. Pour over chicken breasts and serve at once.

I recommend for this dish a hot and tasty garlic, such as Asian Tempest or Rose du Var.

Baleares Chicken

Serves 4

1 (3-pound) chicken, cut in small pieces

Salt and freshly ground black pepper to taste

5 tablespoons olive oil

6 cloves garlic, chopped

1 onion, sliced

1 tablespoon dried thyme

2 cups dry white wine

16 to 18 pitted green olives

1 tablespoon minced fresh parsley

1 bay leaf

Bay leaves, for garnish

Spiral-cut lemon rind, for garnish

Sprinkle chicken with salt and freshly ground pepper to taste. Heat oil in a large, heavy frying pan. Over medium-high heat, brown chicken on all sides for approximately 18 minutes. Transfer chicken to a platter and set aside. Add chopped garlic to frying pan. Reduce heat to medium and add sliced onion. Cook for 6 minutes. Add thyme and continue cooking 1 more minute. Add wine and stir, scraping up leavings on bottom of frying pan.

Bring to a boil for 1 minute. Stir in green olives and parsley. Return chicken pieces to pan, add bay leaf, and reduce heat. Cover and simmer for 20 to 30 minutes, until chicken is done and juices run clear. Transfer chicken to warm serving dish. Let sauce thicken for about 3 minutes. Spoon sauce over chicken and serve at once, garnished with bay leaves and lemon rind, with white rice or sliced, baked ripe plantains.

I recommend for this dish, again, the hot, tasty Asian Tempest garlic or the Rose du Var.

ROSE DU VAR
Softneck Silverskin

Seed from John Swenson via David Cavagnaro at Seed Savers. Originally imported from France by Basic American Foods. Bulb is of a moderate size, with 10 to 14 rose- to-red cloves. Hot, hot, hot.

IL TOSCANO
Allesandro Valentini, Owner

Four years ago, in 1993, I lived for two months in Tuscany, much of the time in Florence. I had tripe dishes not just in Florence but in Rome and Milan, in large and small, elegant and simple, restaurants and trattorias.

Finally, in Florence, I visited il Toscano and knew I'd found, for my taste, the best.

The restaurant was very busy that night and the owner, Allessandro Valentini, could not take the time to have the chef write down the recipe for me. I was returning to the United States the next day, so I left a stamped, self-addressed envelope and requested Signore Valentini, when he had time, to send it to me in California.

It arrived, written in script, two weeks after my return. I am indebted to the Crucianos (Michael, Heather, Michaele, and Chiara) for leading me through the script. They in turn had sought enlightenment from Antonella Arista in Arezzo, who informed them that the one dish her husband refused to eat was trippa.

Most Americans, many Italian-Americans, and even some Italians, cannot stomach

(continued…)

the dish. Like many other dishes based on organs, tripe is a peasant dish born of poverty. Florence has many tripe mobile, *mobile counters*, offering variations of tripe dishes, much like hot dog or coffee carts in the United States.

I was a guest of Sylvia Poggioli and her husband, Piero Benetazzo, in Rome. They took me to their favorite restaurant. When I ordered tripe, Piero was surprised. Was I sure? I was indeed.

After the meal, the owner, a friend of Sylvia and Piero's, came to the table to offer us brandy. He spoke an Italian too rapid for me to follow. "He says you are a special American," Piero translated. "First, you ordered tripe. Second, you ate it all. Third, you used a scarpetta."

Scarpetta is the diminutive of scarpe, *which means shoe. I'd used the heel, or a piece of bread, to soak up the juices and clean my plate.*

RUSSIAN RED STREAK
Softneck Artichoke
(Asiatic strain)

Seed from Filaree Farm. Single-bulb mutation of Russian Red Rocambole. Bulbs moderate to large. Firm, with a long shelf life. In my collection, often exhibits small cloves on neck of stem. Sharp taste in front and roof of mouth as flavor builds.

La Trippa Famosa

Serves 2 to 4

$3/4$ pound tripe

$1/4$ pound *lampredotto**

1 teaspoon salt

1 onion, finely chopped

1 carrot, peeled and finely chopped

1 stalk celery, finely chopped

8 teaspoons olive oil

2 cayenne peppers, finely chopped

2 cloves garlic

8 teaspoons olive oil

2 cups vegetable broth

1 large can whole peeled tomatoes

Salt and freshly ground black pepper
   to taste

Place cold tripe and *lampredotto* in a stockpot over medium-high heat. Add water to cover. Add 1 teaspoon salt and bring to a boil. While water boils, skim off the foam as it forms. Boil for $1 1/2$ hours, drain, and rinse in cold water. (The strong taste of the tripe is removed into the boiling water.) In the stockpot, sauté onion, carrot, celery, and peppers in 8 teaspoons olive oil until soft. Add whole garlic cloves, including the skin. Add salt and pepper to taste. When all is soft, about 10 minutes, cut the tripe into thin slices and add, along with the broth and tomatoes. Again, add salt and pepper to taste. Simmer over medium-low heat, turning often, adding water as necessary to dilute.

Served with grated Parmigiano on top, it looks, as described by Antonella Arista, "…a bit like a plate full of coarsely cut spaghetti with tomato sauce."

For the garlic, use the hot and full and rich Russian Red Streak.

*The stomach of a cow, like Gaul, is divided into 3 parts: the upper (*bomaso*, or in Tuscany, *lampredotto*), the central, most important part (*trippa*), and the end (*millefogli*).

JOANNE WEIR

Joanne Weir is an international cooking teacher and author. The following recipe, Weir writes, "…comes from Stavoula Spyrou, an incomparable cook from Volos, Greece, a fishing village an hour's drive north of Athens."

This spread is the favorite dish of Spyrou's family, Weir says. Spyrou serves it with grilled fish, but it could also accompany grilled chicken or pork tenderloin.

ACROPOLIS
Softneck Artichoke

Seed from Filaree Farm. From Greece. Quite large bulbs and cloves when grown well. Vigorous when well-grown with thick, sturdy stalks. Rich and earthy flavor, with heat at the back of the mouth fading quite soon.

Skorthalia

Makes 1 1/2 cups

1 cup coarsely chopped fresh spinach, washed and dried

1/2 cup fresh bread crumbs

1/4 cup cold water

3/4 cup walnuts, toasted

1/2 cup extra virgin olive oil

4 cloves garlic, minced

1 teaspoon freshly squeezed lemon juice or white wine vinegar

Kosher salt

Freshly ground black pepper to taste

Lemon wedges, for garnish

Bring a pot of salted water to a boil. Add spinach to the boiling water, drain immediately, and set aside. Soak bread crumbs in the cold water and squeeze well to remove excess moisture. Discard the water. Chop walnuts coarsely and reserve 2 tablespoons for garnish. Place spinach, bread crumbs, walnuts, oil, garlic, and lemon juice in a blender or food processor. Blend to a smooth paste. Season to taste with salt and pepper. Spread the paste on a plate. Sprinkle with the reserved walnuts and garnish with lemon wedges.

I recommend for this dish Acropolis garlic, of course, or the mild, slightly sweet California Early.

UNION HOTEL
Lucille Gonnella and the Gonnella Family, Chefs and Proprietors

The first owner of the Union Hotel, Carlo Panizzera, was born in 1889 in Brunia, a small village in the Italian Alps, near Lake Como. He migrated to California in 1917. After working as a cowboy in southern California, he moved to Occidental with enough savings to purchase the Union Saloon, which had opened in the building currently known as the Union Hotel in 1891, shortly after the completion of the North Pacific Coast Railroad.

Each day the narrow-gauge railroad hauled away the local timber and returned with workers, adventurers, and tourists. The Union Saloon became a boarding house and restaurant for the Italian émigrés and the railroad's stopover passengers.

The food and old-world atmosphere began to draw attention from newspapers such as the New York Times *and the* Wall Street Journal.

In 1949 Lucille, the daughter of Carlo and Mary Panizzera, married Dan "Mahoney" Gonnella. Lucille is now president of the Union Hotel. Her son Frank manages the dining room and her daughter-in-law Barbara runs the bakery and the cafe. Lucille's daughter, Mary Theresa, makes the Union Hotel's famous, thick ravioli. Sons Mark and Daniel complete the management team.

The Union Hotel's history is graphically represented in the old and new photographs that cover the walls of cafe, bar, and restaurant. Meals, as in the past hundred years, are very substantial and the prices are low.

Shrimp Pasta

Serves 2

1 tablespoon butter

1 cup manufacturing cream
  (or heavy cream)

$1/4$ cup sliced fresh mushrooms

4 to 6 cloves garlic, freshly peeled
  and chopped

$1/2$ cup clam juice

$1/2$ cup white wine

Salt and freshly ground black pepper to taste

$1/4$ pound shrimp, precooked

$1/2$ pound fettucini, cooked according
  to package directions

Freshly grated Parmesan cheese

In a skillet over medium heat, sauté butter, cream, mushrooms, garlic, clam juice, and wine for 5 minutes. Add salt and pepper to taste. Stir to reduce mixture until it has a thick creamy consistency, about 5 minutes. (Take care not to burn.) Add precooked shrimp, stir into the cream sauce. Serve hot over freshly made fettucini. Top with cheese and serve immediately.

PURPLE GLAZER
Hardneck Purple Stripe

Seed from Filaree Farm, originally from the Republic of Georgia. Large bulb and cloves, both wrapped in satiny skins. Strong, lasting flavor but not hot and no aftertaste.

I recommend for this dish either Gilroy's California Late garlic, which the Union Hotel uses, or the not-quite-so-hot but richer Purple Glazer from the Republic of Georgia.

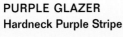

Chicken Polenta

Serves 4 to 6

MARINATED CHICKEN BREASTS

3 cups white wine

2 tablespoons soy sauce

$1/8$ cup brown sugar

4 to 6 cloves garlic, chopped

2 tablespoons olive oil

2 tablespoons chopped fresh rosemary leaves

4 to 6 (5-ounce) chicken breasts

In a baking dish, combine all ingredients and marinate chicken breasts overnight in the refrigerator.

POLENTA

3 quarts water

1 tablespoon salt

3 cups polenta (corn meal)

3 tablespoons butter

Bring salted water to a boil in a large stockpot. Add polenta, stirring constantly. While stirring, add butter. Stir for approximately 15 to 20 minutes until polenta is firm yet still creamy.

FLOHA
Hardneck Porcelain

Seed from Filaree Farm. Originally from Germany. Moderate to large bulb with between 4 and 10 fat brown cloves with colors similar to Purple Stripe. Raw taste, fiery hot. Fine for both roasting and salsa. Long shelf life.

SAUCE FOR CHICKEN AND POLENTA

**4 pounds fresh tomatoes, peeled
    and chopped**

1 red onion, chopped

$1/4$ cup chopped scallons

$1/4$ cup chopped fresh basil

1 tablespoon salt

1 teaspoon freshly ground black pepper

$1/4$ cup butter

$1/4$ cup olive oil

6 to 8 cloves garlic, chopped

$1/2$ cup marsala wine

$1/2$ cup white wine

Preheat oven to 350°. Mix all sauce ingredients in a large casserole and bake for 2 hours, stirring often.

While sauce is baking, prepare a grill and grill marinated chicken breasts for 15 minutes or until meat is no longer pink and the juices run clear.

To serve, place cooked polenta on a serving dish directly from the pot. Make an indentation in the center of polenta. Place sauce in the indentation. Cut the grilled chicken breasts into strips. Place chicken strips on top of sauce. Serve hot.

I recommend for this dish Gilroy's California Late garlic, which the Union Hotel uses, or the Floha garlic from Germany

WIERZYNEK
Edward Szot, Proprietor

The Polish restaurant Wierzynek, near one of the oldest Cracovian sanctuaries, St. Adalbert's Church, is 630 years old.

The towered restaurant began in 1364 with a feast for the wedding of Elisabeth, granddaughter of King Casimir the Great. Guests included kings from twelve countries.

Over the centuries, the restaurant's guest list has included history's most famous and infamous aristocracy. Among those in attendance in recent years have been Haile Selassie, Emperor of Ethiopia; General Charles de Gaulle of France; the Shah of Iran, Reza Pahlavi, and his wife, Farah Diba; Princess Anne of England; Queen Margaret of Denmark; Poland's President Lech Walesa; President Václav Havel of the Czech Republic; President George Bush; France's President Francois-Maurice Mitterand; and Spain's King Juan Carlos with his Queen.

POLISH CARPATHIAN RED
Hardneck Rocambole

Seed from David Cavagnaro and Seed Savers Exchange. Originated in the Carpathian mountains in southeast Poland. Large uniform bulbs. Bulb wrappers covered with thin copper veins and purple blotching. Flavor is hot and spicy, strong and garlicky.

Beef Fillet "Sapieha Style"

Serves 4

1 quart Madeira wine

4 tablespoons strong mustard

1 1/4 teaspoons salt

Freshly ground black pepper to taste

4 thick fillets of beef (about 1/2 pound each)

4 thick slices peasant bread

8 cloves garlic

4 teaspoons butter

4 cups chopped mushrooms (wild, if available; porcini, if possible)

1 cup chopped fresh parsley

In a saucepan, over low heat, simmer the wine for 5 minutes, until it is reduced by half. In a bowl, mix mustard, 1 teaspoon salt, and pepper to taste. Using half the salt-mustard mix, spread top of each fillet with equal amounts. Place fillets on the grill, salt-mustard side down, over hot coals. While meat is grilling, spread remaining portion of mustard mix over top side of meat. Turn steak over when done to the needs of each guest. Once the fillets are turned, spread remaining mix over all fillets. While meat is being prepared, grill 4 slices of bread to toast. Reserve. In a bowl, mix garlic, butter, mushrooms, and remaining salt. Reserve. When grilling is completed, place a fillet on top of each of the slices of toast. Over each hot fillet, spread equal amounts of the garlic butter. Cover each with equal amounts of the reduced madeira sauce. Top each with a heavy pinch of parsley.

Serve with boiled potatoes or potato croquettes and a green salad.

My recommendation for this dish is a sturdy, strong garlic: Polish Carpathian Red, of course.

ZUNI CAFE AND GRILL
Judy Rodgers, Executive Chef

In 1973 as a high school exchange student, Rodgers lived at *Les Frères, with the family of Jean and Pierre Troisgros, noted* cuisiniers à Roanne. *"French kids my age already knew how to make mayonnaise, knew, by taste, where this or that cheese or wine came from." This was a time "…when chefs were just beginning to achieve status.* Newsweek *magazine actually presented Paul Bocuse on its cover."*

Over the next few years, between trips to and from France and Italy, Rodgers worked with chefs Marion Cunningham and Alice Waters.

Executive chef at San Francisco's Zuni for ten years, Rodgers manages 100 employees, including twenty-five cooks. One of her intentions "…is to keep employees interested and motivated."

Though devoted to preparing the finest cuisine, she is also concerned about her world outside the restaurant. One of her special pleasures is Zuni's success in greatly reducing the production of solid waste.

Concerned that rating systems have been unfortunate for cuisines because they tend to make chefs think about status, Rodgers works to make Zuni's food not necessarily different but better, and affordable as well. She does not hesitate to repeat the menus of proven success but, in California, as seasons and offerings vary, Rodgers believes that adjustments in cuisine are not just required, they are inevitable. And challenging.

Quail Cooked with Red Wine and Garlic

(A VARIATION ON COQ AU VIN)

Serves 8

2 tablespoons butter, duck fat, or olive oil

8 fresh whole quail, seasoned with sea salt and refrigerated 24 hours in advance

2 quarts rich chicken stock

1 bottle Pinot Noir or Sangiovese, reduced by half (simmered until it is almost gelatinous)

1 carrot, peeled, halved, and sliced into 1/8-inch half-coins

1 large onion, thinly sliced

1 celery root, peeled and cut into 1/4-inch dice

32 perfect, unpeeled cloves garlic

1 bay leaf

1 sprig fresh thyme

1 sprig parsley

1 handful dried porcini mushrooms, rinsed and then soaked in water until plump and tender

Salt (see below)

3 thick slices bacon, cut into rectangles

Slices of grilled bread

Note: Rodgers feels strongly about the relative use of various kinds of salt available. One teaspoon kosher salt, for example, equals 1/2 teaspoon of sea salt. Finely textured Italian salt is twice as potent as the equal amount of coarse American salt.

Clarify butter in a wide, heavy-bottomed, straight-sided pan by melting over low heat, then skimming off the white that rises to the surface. Brown the quail in the pan. While browning quail, combine stock and wine in a stockpot over medium heat and bring to a simmer. Add vegetables, garlic, herbs, and mushrooms to the browned quail and cook 5 minutes on low-to-moderate heat. There should be no splattering. Begin adding stock/wine mixture a few ounces at a time to the pan, never allowing it to be more than $1/2$ inch deep in bottom of pan. Simmer gently, occasionally turning the quail. The liquid should turn syrupy as it reduces, thinning out as more stock/wine is added. Do not let quail be submerged in braising liquid, and do not let the liquid boil hard.

Note: Not all of stock/wine mixture need be used; the amount depends on size of pan, strength of flame, richness of stock, how "big" the red wine is. Each of these factors affect the rate of evaporation and the amount of reduction that sauce will need.

Adjust salt to taste. After about 30 minutes, the birds, vegetables, and garlic should be tender. If liquid is thin, strain it off into another pan, reduce to velvety consistency, return to pan. Let braising liquid cool completely, up to several hours or even overnight in the refrigerator. (This step is important in rounding the flavors and improving texture.) Just before serving, brown the bacon, discard its fat, and add bacon rectangles to the braise. Bring whole dish back to a simmer. If you like, add a nugget of butter to bind the sauce.

Serve with grilled bread, on which braised garlic cloves may be smeared.

As a fine accompaniment, serve a salad of watercress or chicory with a garlicky vinaigrette.

I recommend for this recipe a zestful, mildly tangy garlic such as Creole Red.

Creole Red

ADDITIONAL VARIETIES

MORADO DE PEDROMERA
Softneck (possible Creole-Silverskin)

From Barcelona via Egmont Tripp, a California garlic grower and collector. First crop shows strain bolting weakly, like hardneck garlics. Small bulbil capsules. Beautiful small-medium bulbs with 2 to 3 layers of striking purple-toned cloves. Sweet- tasting and long-storing.

PORTUGUESE
Hardneck Rocambole

New seed from Sunshine Farms in Cloverdale. Farm owner Tripp found this in a market in Lisbon. Stalks are thin and fernlike, with small bulbs. Taste is a strong and mild.

PURPLE CAULDRON
Softneck Artichoke

Seed from Horace Shaw via Filaree Farm. From Oregon. Bulbs large and vigorous with more purple than many artichoke strains. Long lasting. Stems often produce large, edible, deep dark purple bulbils. Relatively mild flavor.

not pictured

PURPLE TIP
Softneck Purple Stripe

Seed from Dr. Simon via Filaree Farm. One of those garlics considered to have evolved from the original wild garlic of north central Asia. This specific cultivar from Republic of Georgia. Large bulb with large cloves streaked with bright red-purple or light brown. Mild heat but rich flavor.

ROSEWOOD
Hardneck Porcelain

Seed from Russia via Filaree Farm. Moderate to large bulbs with large fat cloves. Smooth, paper-white, tight skins. Hot and pungent with healthy, long-lasting bite. Long-storing.

TRANSYLVANIA:
Softneck Silverskin/Artichoke

Extremely difficult to grow. Small-to-medium-sized heads with 20 to 30 very small, hard-to-peel cloves. Flavor ranges from mild to spicy-hot. Steeped in mystique and history, this is truly a museum garlic.

Garlic Sources

W.A. Burpee
Warminster, PA 18974

Filaree Farm
182 Conconully Hwy.
Okenogan, WA 98840
(free catalog)

Fish Lake Garlic Man
Research and
Experimental Station
RR2
Demoresville, ON
Canada KOK 1WO

Garden City Seeds
1324 Red Crow Road
Victor, MT 59875-9713

Garlic Seed Foundation
Rose Valley Farm
Rose, NY 14542
($10.00 membership includes
growing information and
newsletter.)

Johnny Selected Seeds
Fosshill Rd.
Albion, ME 04910

The Montana Garlic Farm
355 Sunny Dene Rd.
Kalispell, MT 59901

Nichols Nursery
1190 N. Pacific Highway
Albany, OR 97321

Seed Savers Exchange
3076 North Winn Road
Decorah, IA 52101

Seeds Blum
Idaho City Stage
Boise, ID 83706

Seeds of Change
P.O. Box 15700
Santa Fe, NM 87506-5700

Silver Springs Nursery
HCR 62, Box 86
Moyle Springs, ID 83845
(Send SASE for price list.)

Southern Exposure
Seed Exchange
POB 158
North Garden, VA 22959
(catalog $3.00 refundable)

Sunshine Farms
26653 River Road
Cloverdale, CA 95425

Sweetwater Farms
Garlic Division
(Horace Shaw)
Rte. 1, Box 27
Weston, OR 97886
(Send SASE for price list.)

Suggested Readings and References

Aaron, Chester. *Garlic Is Life*. Berkeley, Calif.: Ten Speed Press, 1996.

Anusasananan and Swezey (9/96), "Garlic Revival," *Sunset Magazine*, pp. 80-84.

Brammal, Dr. Ron (1992), "Garlic Production in Ontario—Improved Prospects," Horticultural Experimentation Station, Box 587, Simcoe, Ontario N3Y 4N5.

Brody, Jane (1990), "Garlic Studies," *New York Times*, September 4.

Ciocca, Lyn (1993), "The Nutraceutical *Garlic*," Garlic Seed Foundation *Newsletter*, Summer.

Engeland, Ron L. (1991), *Growing Great Garlic*, Filaree Productions.

Foster, Steven (1991), "Garlic," *Botanical Series* No. 131, American Botanical Council

Fulder, Stephen and John Blackwood (1991), *Garlic—Nature's Original Remedy*, Healing Arts Press.

Kourik, Robert. *Designing and Maintaining Your Edible Landscape Naturally*. Santa Rosa, Calif.: Metamorphic Press, 1986.

—— *Drip Irrigation for Every Landscape and All Climates*. Santa Rosa, Calif.: Metamorphic Press, 1988.

Lawson, Wood, and Hughes (1991), "All About Allicin," *Planta Med.*, Vol. 57, pp. 263-270.

Lawson, Larry, Ph.D. (1993), "Summary of the Cardiovascular Effects of Garlic," Garlic Seed Foundation *Newsletter*, Spring.

Marks, Howard (1991), "Are Garlic Powders as Therapeutic as Raw Garlic?" Garlic Seed Foundation *Newsletter*, Fall.

Poncavage, Joanna (1991), "Grow Great Garlic," *Organic Gardening*, November.

Sanchez, Janet (1992), "Growing and Harvesting Garlic," *Horticulture*, October.

Sreenivasamurthy, V., K. R. Sreekantiah, and D. S. Jonar (1961), "Studies on Stability of Allicin and Aliin Present in Garlic," Central Food Technological Research Institute, Mysore, *J. Sci. Industr. Res.*, Vol. 20, October.

Van Deven, Louis (1992), *Onions and Garlic Forever*, Van Deven.

"Garlic Fights Nitrosamine Formation," *Science News*, Vol. 145, m 12, p 190 (1), March 1994 (author not cited).

"Medical Uses of Garlic—Fact and Fiction" (1982), *Am. Pharm.*, Vol. 22, No. 8.

"Investigation of China's Shipping Garlic at Less Than Fair Value" (1994), Notes: International Trade Administration, *Federal Register*, Vol. 59, No. 131, July 11.

"Market Information on Garlic in Selected European Countries and the United States" (1969), *Report*, International Trade Center, United Nations, Geneva, May.

"The Gift of the Gods." Story of garlic filmed throughout the world on videocassette, 70 minutes. David Douglas Productions Pty Ltd, P.O. Box 97, Cremorne NSW 2090 Australia.

"Garlic Is as Good as Ten Mothers." A videocassette, 50 minutes. Director, Les Blank. Flower Films, 10341 San Pablo Avenue, El Cerrito, CA 94530.

Index